THE RAPE OF THE LOCK

POPE'S
RAPE OF THE LOCK

EDITED BY

GEORGE HOLDEN

OXFORD
AT THE CLARENDON PRESS

OXFORD
UNIVERSITY PRESS
AMEN HOUSE, E.C. 4
London Edinburgh Glasgow New York
Toronto Melbourne Capetown Bombay
Calcutta Madras
HUMPHREY MILFORD
PUBLISHER TO THE
UNIVERSITY

FIRST PUBLISHED 1909
REPRINTED 1912, 1914, 1921, 1924
1927, 1929, 1935, 1936, 1938

PRINTED IN GREAT BRITAIN

PREFATORY NOTE

THIS does not profess to be anything more than a school edition of *The Rape of the Lock*. The text used has been that of Warburton in the nine-volume edition of 1766; this contains Pope's 'last corrections, additions, and improvements', and was 'printed from a copy corrected throughout by the Author himself . . . which, with several additional notes in his own hand, he delivered to the Editor a little before his death'.

Pope's own notes have been reprinted verbatim, and are distinguished by his name.

G. H.

OXFORD : *September,* 1908.

CONTENTS

INTRODUCTION

I

The Rape of the Lock is not merely the most felicitous and characteristic of its author's productions ; an eminent critic has said that, ' taken all in all, it is the most perfect poem in the language.' Lowell, from whom this remark is quoted, did not, of course, mean that Pope's genius was comparable, in what concerns the essentials of poetry, with the greatest or even with many of the secondary names in English literature. Indeed, he commends a criticism of Addison's which ' tacitly excludes him from the position of poet in the highest sense '. But he considers that in this poem Pope, unquestionably a genius in his own kind, found a subject exactly level with his genius. ' As truly as Shakespeare is the poet of man as God made him, dealing with great passions and innate motives, so truly is Pope the poet of society, the delineator of manners, the exposer of those motives which may be called *acquired*, whose spring is in habits and institutions of purely worldly origin.' Or, as another American critic has put it, rather less kindly : ' In *The Rape of the Lock* Pope has caught and fixed for ever the atmosphere of the age . . . no great English poem is at once so brilliant and so empty, so artistic and yet so devoid of the ideals on which all high art rests.'

To understand the possibility of a great poem such as is here described, one must consider the whole character of the age in which Pope lived—a task that cannot in these pages be attempted at any length. It was a time in which society was gradually recovering from the licence which had marked the days of the Stuart Restoration, though the reaction from Puritan times had not yet spent itself; and the civilizing influence of France, a closer connexion with which our country owed to the Restoration, resulted in a veneer of politeness and punctilious etiquette which overlay a good deal of sensualism and brutality. The celebrated *Letters to his Son* of Pope's occasional correspondent, Lord Chesterfield, give an idea, albeit, perhaps, an unduly favourable one, of the social and moral code of the period. The example of the 'Grand Siècle' was everywhere felt, and nowhere more strongly than in the department of literature. A salutary and inevitable reaction against the degenerate Elizabethanism of later Jacobean days had been carried to extravagant lengths in the direction of the worship of correctness, sense, and wit, with a corresponding loss of the 'simple sensuous and passionate' quality which Milton regarded as the essential of poetry. Looking back from a time when the Elizabethan age seems if anything less remote from us in point of feeling than the Augustan, we can nevertheless see the value to English literature of the discipline it then received, and realize how much the poetry, and still more the prose, of the nineteenth century owes to the age of Pope and Addison: we can appreciate the higher qualities it failed to see in what it dismissed as barbarism, and yet do justice to the measure and lucidity it so powerfully imposed on our style, and not unfairly found lacking in its predecessor. But when Pope wrote, Wordsworth, Goethe, Byron, and the whole cataclysm of the French Revolution were undreamed of.

To have given in a single poem what we may call the maximum expression to the social and moral characteristics, the manners and literary taste, of an epoch, is a feat that few have been able to perform.   One might perhaps predicate something of the kind of all truly great writers, in the sense that we feel their works to be at once of their own age and for all time : Dante, Shakespeare, Goethe, presumably could not have been what they were, had not the genius of each found its most congenial and appropriate material in the period and circumstances in which its lot was cast.   But notwithstanding, or perhaps because of, its vastly profounder scope and significance, such a work as *Faust* is far less ' perfect ', in Lowell's sense, than *The Rape of the Lock* : so brilliant, so faithful, and so complete a reflection of an epoch was only possible perhaps on a lower plane, where an artificial style was brought to the description of a correspondingly artificial society and ways of thought.   Such a work must always be in the truest sense unique.

II

The Rape of the Lock is the most dramatic of all Pope's poems.

The story of its origin has been often told.   In the summer of 1711, Robert, the seventh Lord Petre, a young man of twenty-two, had greatly offended his kinswoman, Mistress Arabella Fermor, by cutting off a lock of her hair.   She was already ' an acknowledged beauty ', and not sufficiently nearly related to him for the liberty to be overlooked or pardoned as a youthful frolic, and a quarrel accordingly ensued between the two families.   A friend of Pope's, Mr. John Caryll, who was a second cousin of Lord Petre's, anxious to make peace, suggested to the poet the idea of writing an

amusing poem to ' laugh them out of it ' : this Pope under-
took to do, and *The Rape of the Lock* was the result.

' The first sketch of this poem was written in less than a
fortnight in 1711, in two cantos, and so printed in a Miscellany, without the name of the author. The machines were
not inserted till a year after, when he published it and
annexed the dedication.' [1]

The above are Pope's own words, written in 1736. The
Miscellany to which he refers was a volume of Miscellaneous
Poems by various writers published by Lintot in May, 1712.
The poem was probably written originally in July, 1711, for
there seems to be little doubt that Pope was referring to it
when he wrote to Caryll on August 2 in that year: ' I have
a little poetical present to make you, which I dare not trust
by the post, and could be glad you would please to direct me
a way to send it to you ; for I am a little apprehensive of
putting it into Lewis's [hands], who is too much a bookseller

---

[1] In its first form, the poem consisted of two cantos, of 142 and 192
lines respectively. The first 18 lines of the first canto were substantially
the same as in the enlarged version which was published a year later,
and is the poem as we know it ; then came what are now the first
46 lines of the second canto ; then, the description of Hampton Court,
much the same as at the beginning of what is now the third canto,
as far as line 24 ; then, the description of the coffee-drinking and the
incident which gave rise to the poem, very much as in the subsequent
version, without the ' machinery ' of the Sylphs. The first 10 lines
of canto ii were almost the same as the opening lines of what is now
the fourth canto ; then came what is now line 94, ' The fierce Thalestris,'
&c. ; and the remainder is the same as in the later version, except
for Clarissa's speech (canto v. 7–36), and the allusions to the Sylphs
and Gnomes. It will thus be seen that, in effect, the portions added
by Pope for the enlarged version consist of the ' machinery ' of the
Sylphs and Gnomes, and the incidents connected with it ; the account
of Belinda's toilette ; the short voyage on the Thames ; the game of
Ombre ; and the pedigree of the bodkin. The speech of Clarissa
(canto v. 7–36) was added for the first time in the collected edition of
Pope's works published in 1717.

to be trusted with rhyme or reputation.' (The Lewis mentioned was W. Lewis, a bookseller of Russell Street, Covent Garden, who had published Pope's *Essay on Criticism* earlier in the same year.) Part of the leaf at the bottom of the sheet is worn away, so that we do not know what followed after the word 'reputation'; but that it was *The Rape of the Lock* in its original form is more than probable, for in the following May (1712) Pope says, in another letter to Caryll: 'But where hangs the Lock now? Though I know that, rather than draw any just reflection upon yourself of the least shadow of ill-nature, you would freely have suppressed one of the best of poems. I hear no more of it : will it come out in Lintot's *Miscellany* or not ? I wrote to Lord Petre on the subject of the Lock some time since, but have as yet had no answer.'

The date assigned by Pope himself to the last-mentioned letter is May 23, 1712. Lintot's *Miscellany* was certainly published at the latest within two days from that date, for Mr. Edward Bedingfield wrote acknowledging the receipt of copies to be given to Lord Petre and to Arabella Fermor on May 26, and on May 28 Pope himself writes again to Caryll, 'I hope Lewis has conveyed you by this time *The Rape of the Lock*, with what other things of mine are in Lintot's collection. . . . Mr. Bedingfield . . . has done me the favour to send some books of the Rape to my Lord Petre and Mrs. Fermor.' It would seem to be fairly clear that Pope was not then personally acquainted with either Miss Fermor or with Lord Petre, and that Warburton, who was what we should nowadays call Pope's 'literary executor', was mistaken in his statement that he was acquainted with the lady and that 'she took it so well as to give about copies of it'. Warburton goes on to point to the motto, adapted from an epigram of Martial,[1] which Pope had prefixed to the poem, as implying that it ' was written or published at the lady's request '. But Elwin shows that this was not so. It was not *written* at her request, for she could not have suggested to any one to write a poem to laugh her out of her own very natural resentment against Lord Petre, and we have moreover Pope's own words (canto i. 3) that ' this verse ' was ' due to Caryll '. Neither can it have been *published* at her request ; for, in his introductory letter to Miss Fermor prefixed to the enlarged version, Pope, speaking of the first edition, says, ' an imperfect copy having been offered to a bookseller, you had the good nature for my sake to consent to the publication of one more correct.' There is, however, a piece of evidence still stronger, contained in the poem itself. In canto iv. 169, Pope speaks of Arabella's hair as ' sable ringlets '. Now, there are three more or less authenticated portraits of the lady in existence (to which we shall refer presently), and in each of them the long curling locks are shown, and in all three she has fair auburn hair. This would seem to prove that Pope was not personally acquainted, at all events, with Miss Fermor, when *The Rape of the Lock* was originally written.

With regard to the motto from Martial, Pope substituted for this in the enlarged edition (1714) part of a line from Ovid's *Metamorphoses* (see note to canto iii. 122) which could convey no such implication as that suggested by Warburton : though, it is true, the original motto was replaced when the poem was reprinted in the ' Collected Works ' (1717).

---

[1] Mr. Courthope, in his *Life of Pope* (p. 93), says that Martial's epigram also suggested the name of the heroine ; but the epigram (xii. 84) is addressed to one Polytimus.

III

And now it is time to give some account of the various people above mentioned ; and first of the poet himself.

1. Alexander Pope was a Roman Catholic, as were all the persons with whom we shall be concerned. There is authority for supposing that his grandfather was a clergyman of the Church of England, the Rev. Alexander Pope, Rector of Thruxton in Hampshire. His son (also called Alexander), the father of the poet, was placed by his father in a merchant's house of business at Lisbon, and there became a Roman Catholic. When he was over forty years of age, he married, for his second wife, Edith Turner, the daughter of a Yorkshire gentleman ; his first wife, 'Magdelen,' having died in 1679, in Broad Street in the city of London, where he was in business as a linendraper. After his second marriage he moved into Lombard Street, and there the poet was born on May 21, 1688.

On the authority of the poet's half-sister, Mrs. Rackett, we are told of an accident that happened to her brother when he was about three years old. 'He was filling a little cart with stones, a cow struck at him, carried off his hat and feather with her horns, and flung him down on the heap of stones he had been playing with. In the fall he cut himself against one of them, in his neck, near the throat.'

In those days Roman Catholics had some difficulty in getting their sons educated in England, for they were forbidden by law to keep a school, and the two Universities were of course closed to them. Young Pope's first teacher seems to have been ' an old aunt ', who taught him to read, and he taught himself to write by copying printed books.

When he was about eight years old he was entrusted to the care of the family priest, a Jesuit of the name of Banister, who began to teach him Latin and Greek simultaneously, after the fashion of the time. His first school, according to the most recent authority,[1] seems to have been that set up by Thomas Deane in Marylebone, and afterwards removed to Hyde Park Corner. This Thomas Deane, *alias* Thomas Franks, S.J., *alias* Father Francis, had been deprived of his fellowship at University College, Oxford, in February, 1688, and coming to London had been imprisoned on account of his religion, and in 1691 had (under the above *aliases*) stood in the pillory at Charing Cross. The school eventually collapsed, and poor Deane fell upon evil times. He was confined in the Fleet prison for debt in 1727, when his old pupil, Pope, came forward to help him, and gave him a small pension which was continued till his death in 1735. It was while at Deane's school that young Pope composed a little tragedy made up of speeches out of Ogilby's translation of Homer and lines written by himself. The play was acted by Pope and his schoolfellows, and Mr. Deane's gardener was 'pressed' to perform the part of Ajax. According to the authority above referred to, it was here, too, that the lad composed a satire[2] upon his master, for which he was flogged, and this led to his being removed from the school and sent to Twyford near Winchester. This last-named school had originally been founded at Silksteed by the Rev. Augustine Taylor, and was removed to Twyford at his death in 1692. It was the

---

[1] Mrs. Bryan Stapleton, whose account of Pope's schooldays is considerably at variance with that given in Mr. Courthope's *Life*, and in Spence's *Anecdotes* and other authorities. (See her *History of the Post-Reformation Catholic Missions in Oxfordshire*. London, 1906.)

[2] According to Pope's half-sister, Mrs. Rackett, this occurred at Twyford and not at Mr. Deane's school.

only Roman Catholic school that survived the Reformation. The master in Pope's day was a Mr. Taverner, who subsequently became chaplain at Warkworth Castle, near Banbury, where he died in 1745.

When Pope was twelve years old, his father left London and went to live at Binfield in Windsor Forest. There the boy was placed under the care of yet another priest, and, to use his own words, ' This was all the teaching I ever had, and, God knows, it extended a very little way.' 'When I had done with my priests,' he said to Spence, ' I took to reading by myself, for which I had a very great eagerness and enthusiasm, especially for poetry. . . . I continued in this close pursuit of pleasure and languages till nineteen or twenty. . . . I went through all the best critics; almost all the English, French, and Latin poets of any name; the minor poets, Homer, and some of the greater Greek poets, in the original; and Tasso and Ariosto in translations. I even then liked Tasso better than Ariosto, as I do still; and Statius of all the Latin poets by much next to Virgil.'

We have referred thus fully to the subject of Pope's education, as it is of especial interest in connexion with the poem with which we have to do. *The Rape of the Lock* has been well called a ' mosaic of quotations, parodies, and allusions, derived from the masters of epic and narrative poetry'.[1] Fully to appreciate these allusions would require a wider and more familiar knowledge of classical literature than most of us possess nowadays. Not but what our knowledge of the classics is deeper and more accurate than was that of our forefathers ; but that knowledge is not nearly so widely distributed either amongst the classics or amongst

[1] Ryland, *The Rape of the Lock*, Introduction, **p. liv.**

ourselves as it was then. The education of the eighteenth-century gentleman was founded almost exclusively on the classics ; and rhythm, thoughts, words, forms of phrase, and allusions had a meaning for him which may well be missed by the reader of average culture to-day. Homer, and Virgil, and Horace we know more or less, but who reads Statius now? The charm which *The Rape of the Lock* has for us is therefore different from that which it possessed for contemporary readers. We are more attracted by the vivid picture of fashionable life two hundred years ago.

Even as regards the mere language of the poem, our attention is engaged in a different manner. It is not the echoes of Homer and Virgil which attract us so much as the flavour of anticlimax, unexpected trope, and epigram. It would be almost true to say that in this ' Heroi-comical ' poem it is the comical part which makes most appeal to us, as the heroic part did to our ancestors. This is, however, a mere matter of detail after all ; and, as Mr. Courthope puts it, ' the pleasure with which the poem is read in the reign of Queen Victoria is the same *in kind* as that with which it was read in the reign of Queen Anne.' It is, to say the least, noteworthy that a poem so abounding in classical allusion should have been the work of a lad like Pope, almost entirely self-educated, and to whom the ordinary advantages of his time were, as we have seen, in large measure denied.

It was at Binfield that the boy's health first began to suffer from his too assiduous study. He had an attack of melancholia which led him to imagine that he was about to die, and he wrote farewell letters to several of his acquaintance, one of whom, the Abbé Southcote, consulted Dr. John Radcliffe, the most famous doctor of the day, about his young friend's health. Radcliffe prescribed rest, a changed diet, and a daily ride through Windsor Forest, and so succeeded for a time in restoring his health and spirits. This perpetual study, however, says his cousin, Mr. Mannick, was the cause of his subsequent ill health ; it ' changed his form, and ruined his constitution '. Thackeray gives us a touching picture : ' his body was crooked : he was so short that it was necessary to raise his chair in order to place him on a level with other people at table. He was sewed up in a buckram suit every morning, and required a nurse like a child ' ; and he alludes in a note to his being fed on ass's milk, and to his (Pope's) own lines about his friend Dr. Arbuthnot having helped him through ' that long disease, my life'.

It was during the Binfield days, too, that Pope made many of his friends. His first poet-friend was probably Wycherley, the dramatist, who would send him his verses to correct. Another was the minor poet, William Walsh, with whom he spent much of the summer of 1705 at his home in Worcester-shire. Another constant companion was Sir William Trum-bull, of Easthampstead Park, a retired diplomatist, who had been a Fellow of All Souls College, Oxford, and ' who ', says Pope, ' loved very much to read and talk of the Classics in his retirement. We used to take a ride out together three or four days in the week, and at last almost every day.' Of Walsh, Pope said, in later life, ' He used to encourage me much, and used to tell me that there was one way left of excelling ; for though we had several great poets, we never had one great poet that was correct, and he desired me to make that my study and aim.' Mr. Courthope points out that by ' correctness ' Walsh meant not only accuracy of expression, but also propriety of design and justice of thought and taste.

Pope's first published poems were the *Pastorals*, the *Imitation of Ovid's ' Sappho Phaoni'*, and that of Chaucer's *Merchant's Tale (January and May)*, all of which appeared, together with poems by Rowe, Swift, Wycherley, Ambrose Philips, and others, in a volume of *Poetical Miscellanies*, published by Jacob Tonson in 1709. Philips's contribution to this volume was also ' Pastorals'; as to this, see the note to Canto iii. 19, 20. Mr. Courthope says that ' it may be safely assumed that the idea of Pope's *Pastorals* was the fruit of' his friendship and intercourse with Sir William Trumbull. Pope himself said that the *Pastorals* had been written as early as 1704; they had been shown to many of his friends besides Sir William Trumbull, to whom the first was dedicated, such as Henry Cromwell, Lord Halifax, Wycherley, Congreve, Garth, and others. Sir George Granville, afterwards Lord Lansdowne, wrote of ' a young poet . . . whom he [Wycherley] and Walsh have taken under their wing. His name is Pope . . . If he goes on as he has begun in the Pastoral way . . . we may hope to see English poetry vie with the Roman.' Tonson himself had seen one of these Pastorals in 1706, and had asked to be allowed to publish it.

About the same time, according to Pope's own account, he wrote the first 290 lines of his *Windsor Forest*, but the latter portion was not written till 1710, and the poem itself was not published till 1713. His next publication was the *Essay on Criticism*, which was written either in 1707 or 1709 (it is not clear which), and was published in May, 1711. This was noticed favourably in *The Spectator* for December 20 in the same year, and Pope wrote a grateful letter of acknowledgement to Steele, whom he assumed to have been the writer of the article. Steele replied that the paper was not written by him, but ' by one with whom I will make you acquainted, which is the best return I can make to you'. This was the beginning of Pope's acquaintance with Addison, who published Pope's poem *The Messiah* in *The Spectator* for the 14th of the following May. In the same month appeared the first version of *The Rape of the Lock*, which—as we have seen—was written in the previous July. Pope was then twenty-three years old, and had already made his mark as a poet.

2. His friend and correspondent, John Caryll, was, in 1711, double Pope's age, having been born in or about 1666. The son of Mr. Richard Caryll of West Grinstead in Sussex, he had succeeded to his father's property there on the latter's death in 1701. But he had also property (Lady Holt) of his own at West Harting in the same county. This had come to him as the grantee of the forfeited estates of his uncle (also John Caryll), who had been secretary to James II's Queen Mary ; he had followed her into France, and had been made 'Baron Caryll of Dunford' by the Old Pretender at the Court of St. Germains. Macaulay was confusing him with his nephew when he wrote, ' Half a line in *The Rape of the Lock* has made his name immortal.' He never returned to England, and died in Paris at the age of eighty-six on September 4, 1711, before *The Rape of the Lock* was published. He had left England in the year in which Pope was born, so that he could not have been the inspirer of the poem. No doubt Pope was well acquainted with many members of the Caryll family, as is evidenced by a couplet in Gay's poem *Pope's Welcome from Greece*—

I see the friendly Carylls come by dozens,
Their wives, their uncles, daughters, sons, and cousins.

But it cannot be doubted that his especial friend and the

inspirer of *The Rape of the Lock* was John Caryll, the nephew
His intimacy and correspondence with Pope lasted from
1710 till his (Caryll's) death in 1736. His grandmother had
been a daughter of the second Lord Petre, so that he was
a second cousin to ' The Baron ' of the poem.

3. Robert, seventh Lord Petre (*The Baron*), was about
a year younger than Pope, having been born in the early
part of 1689. He had succeeded his father in the title some
three years before he was guilty of the Rape of Miss Fermor's
Lock, and was at the time a young man of twenty-two. He
married Miss Catharine Walmesley in the following March,
before the publication of the first version of the poem, and
died in the next year of small-pox.

4. We now come to the central figure of the story, Miss
Arabella Fermor (*Belinda*).

Sir Richard Fermor of Somerton in Oxfordshire had died
in 1642, leaving eight children. It is only with two of these
that we are concerned : firstly, his daughter Lucy, who
married William, the second surviving son of the second Lord
Petre, and a brother of the Lady Catharine Petre who had
married John Caryll's grandfather, so that she was a great-
aunt to Robert, the seventh Lord Petre (*The Baron*), as well
as Caryll's grandmother; secondly, his son Henry, who was
the grandfather of Mr. Henry Fermor of Tusmore and
Somerton, the father of Arabella. The last-named Henry
Fermor married ' Hellen ',[1] the second daughter of Sir
George Browne of Wickham Breux in Kent.[2] They had nine
children : two sons, James and Henry, and seven daughters,

[1] So called in her husband's will, and also on the monument at
Somerton, where she was buried in 1741.

[2] The Baronetage mentions her as the daughter of Sir George Browne
of Caversham, K.B. This is the same family ; but Sir George was not
a Baronet. It was his brother John who was created a Baronet in 1665.

f whom Arabella was the eldest.[1] Her age in 1711 cannot
vith certainty be fixed, but it was probably about nineteen
r twenty. The evidence of this is as follows:[2]—

In April, 1700, Henry Fermor (Arabella's father) charged
he family property with portions for his daughters, Arabella's
ortion being three times as large as those of her younger
isters. These portions were to become payable at the age
f twenty-one or earlier marriage, and in the meantime
'maintenance' was to be paid for each daughter of £30
·er annum until they should respectively reach the age of
hirteen, and of £50 per annum afterwards.

[1] Mr. Courthope in his *Life of Pope* (1889) says that she 'was the
ourth child of Henry, the proprietor of the place, and of Alice (sic)
is wife'. This is, I think, a mistake: and perhaps is to be accounted
or by the fact that she is shown as the fourth child in the Fermor
edigree, printed in the *Genealogical Collections illustrating the
History of Roman Catholic Families of England. Based on the Lawson
Manuscript. Part I, edited by J. Jackson Howard and H. Farnham
Burke. Printed for Private circulation only*, 1887. There are other
nistakes in this pedigree, of which there are two copies in the Bodleian
Library at Oxford, one of them being entitled as above, and the other
aving no title-page, but acquired by the Library in 1880.

N.B. If the order of the daughters given in the 'Howard and Burke'
edigree is right, Arabella *could* not have been more than fifteen, if so
uch, at the time when the outrage was committed; and at that age
he would not have been styled Mrs. (Mistress), nor is she likely to have
een 'an acknowledged beauty'.

[2] In the year 1856, Sir Charles Robert Tempest petitioned the House
f Lords for the determination in his favour of the abeyance into which
he Barony of de Scales had fallen at the end of the fifteenth century,
laiming to prove that he had vested in him one 72nd part of one
noiety of the said Barony! Mr. Chester Waters in his *Chesters of
Chicheley* shows that the descent of one moiety is wholly misrepresented
n the minutes of evidence printed for this claim (see Cokayne's *Peerage*,
.v. de Scales), which was rejected by the House of Lords in 1856. But,
owever untrustworthy in matters of pedigree the de Scales evidence
nay be, there were many deeds, connected with the Fermor family,
roduced by the late Mr. Clement Uvedale Price, the family lawyer,
nd these were set out at length in the evidence, and speak for them-
elves. It is on the contents of some of these deeds that the statements
n the text are founded.

The daughters mentioned in this deed are in the following order : Arabella, Winifred, Mary Ursula, Anne, Henrietta and Hellen (Elizabeth was not born then ; a similar provision was made for her by a later deed dated in 1702).

Henry Fermor's eldest son, James, married Miss Mary Throckmorton in 1713, and one of the deeds connected with the settlement made upon his marriage describes Arabella as ' the eldest sister of the said James Fermor ' ; furthermore she alone of all the sisters is a ' party ' to this deed, which bears date July 11, 1713. This deed fully ' recites ' the ' portion-deed ' of 1700, mentioned above, and goes on to state that Arabella's portion thereunder had ' become payable ' It would seem, therefore, to be clear that (1) Arabella was not yet thirteen years old in 1700, and (2) that she *was* twenty-one years old in 1713. This means that she was born between the years 1687 and 1692. There is no evidence forthcoming to fix the date of her birth more closely, but the probabilities would seem to be that one at least of her two brothers was older than she (they are both of them ' parties ' to the deed of 1713), and the later date is perhaps the most likely. The order in which the daughters are named varies somewhat in the two deeds, and in that of 1713 Henrietta is called Herriott, but Arabella heads the list in both.

This would seem to be a convenient place for enumerating the nine children of Henry Fermor and Hellen his wife ; they were as follows :—

1. James, the eldest son, who married Miss Throckmorton in 1713.

2. Henry, the younger son, who married Miss Wightwick of Banbury, and died in 1736.

3. Arabella, who married Francis Perkins of Ufton Court, and with whom we are now concerned.

4. Winifred, a nun, became abbess at Dunkirk ; name in religion, Frances.

5. Mary Ursula, a nun ; name in religion, Placida.

6. Anne, who married John Sutton of Jamaica, and died in 1749.

7. Henrietta, who died unmarried in 1744, æt. 49.

8. Hellen, who died an infant prior to 1713.

9. Elizabeth, a nun, born in 1702.

With regard to the last-named, Elizabeth, the 'Howard and Burke' pedigree states that she was born in 1702, and that is the year in which the deed providing for her portion is dated. It is somewhat strange that her 'act of profession', which bears date November 21, 1716, should state that she was then 'ætatis anno 18'. This would make the year of her birth 1698, which could not have been the case, for the deed of 1713 states distinctly that she was born 'since the making of the said recited Indenture' of 1700.

Whether Mr. Courthope's words that 'both Arabella Fermor and Lord Petre were prominent members in Roman Catholic Society' are accurate is open to doubt, but that she was 'an acknowledged beauty' at a comparatively early age is borne out by Miss Mitford's words in *The Ladies' Companion* for August 10, 1850. Speaking of Ufton Court, she says :—

'Fifty years ago a Catholic priest was the sole inhabitant of this interesting mansion. His friend, the late Mrs. Lenoir, Christopher Smart's daughter, . . . wrote some verses to the great oak. Her nieces, whom I am proud to call my friends, possess many reliques of that lovely Arabella Fermor, of whom Pope, in the charming dedication to the most charming of his poems, said that " the character of Belinda . . . resembled her in nothing but beauty ". Among these reliques are her rosary, and a portrait, taken when she was twelve or thirteen years of age. The face is most interesting : a high, broad forehead ; dark eyes, richly fringed and deeply set ; a straight nose, pouting lips, and a short chin finely rounded. The dress is dark and graceful, with a little white turned back about the neck, and the loose sleeves. Altogether, I never saw a more charming girlish portrait, with so much of present beauty, and so true a promise of more; of that order, too, high and intellectual, which great poets love. Her last surviving son died childless in 1769, and the estate passed into another family.'

This portrait, which was exhibited at the Pope Commemoration at Twickenham in 1888, is reproduced in Miss Sharp's *History of Ufton Court* (4° : London, 1892), where it is stated to be then in the possession of Mr. W. W. Cowslade, of Earley, near Reading. Miss Sharp also gives two other portraits of Arabella; one, which is said to be the next in point of date, belonging to her descendant (collateral, doubtless, as none of her sons had issue), Colonel Sir Ivor Herbert, Bt., of Llanarth, who 'also has the companion portrait of her husband'. These two pictures were probably painted soon after her marriage. She is depicted as young and very charming ; two long curling locks resting on her shoulders, and round her neck the cross ' which Jews might kiss and infidels adore '. The third portrait given in Miss Sharp's book, belonged, she says, to ' Mrs. Welby-Parry, having formed part of the collection of the late Mr. Hartley of Bucklebury. It is said to be by Sir Godfrey Kneller, and its artistic merits quite bear out the supposition. It is of a woman in the prime of her beauty and grace ; the pose is very elegant, and the colour charming ; in it she still wears the fashionable love-lock of the day. All three portraits have much individuality and many points of resemblance.

Hair of a warm golden shade, a slender neck and sloping shoulders, almond-shaped eyes with well-formed level eyebrows, are characteristic of them all. In fact, . . . the representations of beauty which artists have handed down to us fully bear out the praises of contemporary writers.'

Arabella Fermor was married to Francis Perkins, Esquire, of Ufton Court, in Berkshire, in 1714, or very early in 1715.[1] This is proved by a post-nuptial settlement made upon her by her husband in June, 1715, which is expressed to be made between ' Francis Perkins of Ufton Court and Arabella his wife of the first part, &c.' One of the trustees of this settlement was William, Lord Stawell, who was Gentleman of the Bedchamber to George, Prince of Denmark, the Prince Consort ; and the deed gives the portion which Arabella brought her husband at her marriage as £4,500.

Pope had written her a charming letter of congratulation on her marriage, of which we have not space to quote more than one sentence. ' You are now,' he writes, ' a married woman, and in a way to be a great many better things than a fine lady ; such as an excellent wife, a faithful friend, a tender parent, and, at last, as the consequence of them all, a saint in heaven.'

There were four children of the marriage, all sons, viz :—

Francis, who died unmarried in 1750.

James, who died unmarried in 1755.

Charles, who died unmarried in 1762.

John, who died without issue in 1769.

[1] The date 1714 is (on the authority of Croker) prefixed by Elwin to Pope's letter to Martha Blount in which he says ' It was but the other day I heard of Mrs. Fermor's being actually and directly married ' ; and also to the letter from Pope to Mrs. Arabella Fermor on her marriage. The ' Howard and Burke ' pedigree has 1736 as the date of Arabella's marriage, but the mistake is pointed out.

Mr. Perkins died in 1736; his widow survived him only two years, and was buried at Ufton on March 9, 173$\frac{7}{8}$.

5. *Sir Plume*, Belinda's champion in the poem, has been identified by many authorities, including Burke and Mrs. Bryan Stapleton, with George, the only son of Sir Charles Browne of Kiddington, in Oxfordshire. It is likely enough that this George Browne may have been acquainted with the lady, for they were neighbours. Indeed, in after years he married, for his third wife, the widow (née Frances Sheldon) of Arabella's nephew Henry ; [1] but in 1711 he was only a lad of seventeen, and moreover did not become ' Sir George Browne ' till some forty years afterwards. It is more likely that the Sir George Browne meant was Sir George Browne of Caversham, who was a first cousin of Arabella's mother, and who had succeeded to his brother's title in 1692. It is not clear what his age was in 1711, but he cannot have been very young, as two of his brothers had preceded him in the Baronetcy. Spence says that the description of him in *The Rape of the Lock* was ' The very picture of the man '. He had been an officer in the Austrian service, and had married, as his first wife, Gertrude Morley, a sister of John Morley, the ' land-jobber ' (Swift's ' rascally butcher '), who was a friend of Pope's in later years.

6. This John Morley had himself married Sir George's sister Elizabeth, and it is she who figures as *Thalestris* in the poem. Her age in 1711 is also a matter for conjecture.

The accompanying pedigree will serve, it is hoped, to make the various relationships more clear to the reader.

---

[1] It is this lady to whom Horace Walpole refers in a letter to Miss Mary Berry of August 17, 1796: ' So you found a picture of your predecessor ! She had had a good figure; but I had rather it had been a portrait of her aunt, Mrs. Arabella Fermor, the heroine of the Lock, of whom I never saw a resemblance.'

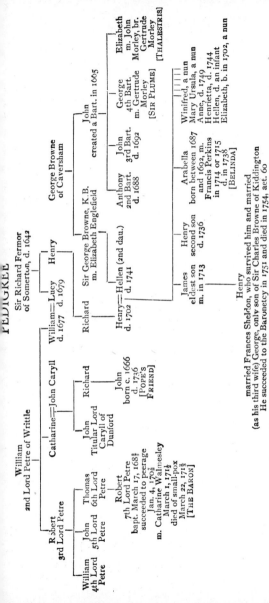

PEDIGREE

Sir Richard Fermor of Somerton, d. 1642

William—2nd Lord Petre of Writtle

Catharine=John Caryll

William d. 1677 — Lucy d. 1679 — Henry

George Browne of Caversham

Sir George Browne, K.B. m. Elizabeth Englefield

John created a Bart. in 1665

Robert 3rd Lord Petre

John Titular Lord Caryll of Dunford

Richard

Richard

Henry=Hellen (2nd dau.) d. 1741

Anthony 2nd Bart. d. 1688

John 3rd Bart. d. 1692

George 4th Bart. m. Gertrude Morley [SIR PLUME]

Elizabeth m. John Morley, br. Gertrude Morley [THALESTRIS]

William 4th Lord Petre

John 5th Lord Petre

Thomas 6th Lord Petre

John born c. 1666 d. 1736 [POPE'S FRIEND]

Henry=Hellen d. 1702

Henry

married Frances Sheldon, who survived him and married
(as his third wife) George, only son of Sir Charles Browne of Kiddington
He succeeded to the Baronetcy in 1751 and died in 1754, aet. 60

James eldest son m. in 1713

Henry second son d. 1736

Arabella born between 1687 and 1692, m. Francis Perkins in 1714 or 1715 d. in 1738 [BELINDA]

Winifred, a nun
Mary Ursula, a nun
Anne, d. 1749
Henrietta, d. 1744
Hellen, d. an infant
Elizabeth, b. in 1702, a nun

Robert 7th Lord Petre bapt. March 17, 1688¾ succeeded to peerage Jan. 4, 170⁴⁄₅ m. Catharine Walmesley March 1, 171¾ died of small-pox March 22, 171⁸⁄₉ [THE BARON]

N. B. Except in the case of Arabella and her brothers and sisters, families are not given in their entirety in the above pedigree. We are concerned, for instance, only with the descendants of three of the children of William (the Baron of the Poem), viz.: his eldest son, who was the second Lord Petre, was the grandfather of Robert, seventh Lord (Pope's friend, who suggested the poem); secondly, his daughter, Catharine, who married John Caryll, and became the grandmother of John Caryll (Pope's friend, who suggested the poem); thirdly, his second surviving son, William, who married Lucy Fermor, sister of Henry Fermor, the great-grandfather of Arabella (the Belinda of the Poem). It will be seen that Arabella's mother was a daughter of Sir George Browne, K.B., whose brother John was made a Baronet in 1665; the latter being succeeded by three of his sons in succession (George, the fourth Baronet, who married Gertrude Morley, being the Sir Plume of the Poem). Sir John Browne had also a daughter, Elizabeth, who married John Morley, brother of Gertrude, and she is the Thalestris of the Poem.

IV

The first version of *The Rape of the Lock* did not meet with warm welcome from the Fermor family. In after years, indeed, Pope told Spence that 'it was well received and had its effect in the two families. Nobody but Sir George Browne was angry, and he was a good deal so, and for a long time. He could not bear that Sir Plume should talk nothing but nonsense.' But he was speaking of the enlarged version; and he himself wrote to Caryll on November 8, 1712, 'Sir Plume blusters, I hear; nay, the celebrated lady herself is offended, and, which is stranger, not at herself, but me.'

The offended attitude of the Fermors can be readily understood and appreciated, and it was perhaps the real cause of the enlarged version of the poem, which seems to have been written with the idea, on Pope's part, of rendering it less personal, and so propitiating the family. In this he would appear to have at all events partly succeeded. Thus on December 15, 1713, he writes to Caryll, 'I have been employed, since my being here in the country, in finishing the additions to *The Rape of the Lock*, a part of which I remember I showed you. I have some thoughts of dedicating that poem to Mrs. Fermor by name, as a piece of justice in return to the wrong interpretations she has suffered on the score of that piece.' And, a month later, 'As to *The Rape of the Lock*, I believe I have managed the dedication so nicely that it can neither hurt the lady nor the author. I writ it very lately, and upon great deliberation. The young lady approves of it, and the best advice in the kingdom, of the men of sense, has been made use of in it, even to the Treasurer's [Lord Oxford]. A preface which salved the lady's honour, without affixing her name, was also prepared, but by herself

uperseded in favour of the dedication. Not but that, after
ll, fools will talk, and fools will hear them.'

The foregoing passages enable us to read between the lines
f the Introductory Letter, and especially of the two con-
:luding paragraphs. There is next to no evidence forth-
:oming as to how far the family indignation was allayed ;
.hey probably, having nominally forgiven the offence, still
etained a subdued feeling of annoyance, as is reflected in the
vords of Dr. Johnson, who says, ' Whether all this be true
 have some doubt ; for at Paris, a few years ago [he was
vriting in 1778] a niece of Mrs. Fermor, who presided in an
English convent,[1] mentioned Pope's work with very little
gratitude, rather as an insult than an honour ; and she
nay be supposed to have inherited the opinion of her
amily.'[2]

Be this, however, as it may, there is no question but what
he enlarged version was well received by the public. Ten
lays after it appeared Pope informed Caryll that 3,000
:opies had been sold in four days, and that it was already
reprinted '. Pope, who had received £7 from Lintot for
he first version, was paid a further sum of £15.

The next step upon Pope's part is somewhat curious. It
s conceivable that it may have been in some degree a device
or mending matters still further with the Fermors, or it
nay have been merely an attempt on the part of Pope to
eed the interest which the poem had excited in a surrep-
itious manner, for he delighted in such tortuous proceedings,
|uite apart from the point of view of mere gain. But, how-
:ver this may be, in the following year there appeared a

[1] Two of Arabella's nieces, Bridget and Frances, were Augustine nuns
n Paris in 1781. Frances, whose name in religion was Mary Agnes,
lied at the age of 76, on March 9, 1794.
[2] Boswell's *Johnson*, ed. G. Birkbeck Hill, ii. 392.

pamphlet entitled, *A Key to the Lock, or a Treatise proving, beyond all contradiction, the dangerous Tendency of a late poem, entitled, ' The Rape of the Lock,' to Government and Religion, by Esdras Barnivelt, Apoth.* This had prefixed to it several commendatory verses, after the fashion of the day ; and also an ' Epistle dedicatory to Mr. Pope ', in which *The Rape of the Lock* is referred to as ' the poison which hath been so artfully distilled through your guile, and conveyed to the world through the pleasing vehicle of your numbers ', and ' the uncommon sale of this book (for above 6,000 of 'em have been already vended) was also a further reason that called aloud upon me to put a stop to its further progress.'

This was written by Pope himself,[1] and apparently had been some time in contemplation. The matter of the *Key to the Lock* may be summarized as follows :—' Mr. Barnivelt ' says : ' I consider it to be my duty to warn the public against *The Rape of the Lock*. The author, as we all know, is a Papist, and may well have been corrupted by the Jesuits, although, generally speaking, he is level-headed enough. Now, Papists know that the publication of books tending to propagate their doctrines is dangerous, so they are obliged to disguise their productions. They know, too, that in England the Church and the State are so firmly united that attacking one is attacking the other. Though I cannot positively affirm that *The Rape of the Lock* was intended to spread Roman Catholic ideas, I am led to think so by the fact that many Roman Catholics have appropriated the various characters in the poem to themselves. For instance, Sir Plume and

---

[1] Swift writes from Dublin to Pope on June 28, 1715: ' I saw the *Key to the Lock* but yesterday : I think you have changed it a good deal to adapt it to present times.'

Belinda (the last-named in spite of the disclaimer contained in the dedication).

' Looked at from a political point of view, if we may assume, as we may do, that by the Lock itself is symbolized the Barrier Treaty,[1] then we have Belinda representing Great Britain, or (which is the same thing) Queen Anne herself; the Baron, who cuts off the Lock (the Barrier Treaty), is the Earl of Oxford; Clarissa, who lent the scissors, is my Lady Masham; Thalestris, who resents the loss of the Lock, or Treaty, is the Duchess of Marlborough;[2] Sir Plume is Prince Eugene; the Sylphs and Gnomes are the two rival political parties, Ariel being Lord Oxford, and Umbriel some other " grave and worthy minister "; Zephyretta, Brillante, and the rest, are the Queen's ladies; the wounded Sylph is Lord Townshend; the pet dog " Shock " is Dr. Sacheverell; and the line about the power of " unresisted steel " (canto iii. 178) is a punning allusion to the poet's friend Richard Steele, of *The Tatler*. Furthermore, by the game of Ombre is meant the late war, in which Belinda (Britain) plays against

[1] The Barrier Treaty, which was signed in November 1715, was the embodiment of an agreement come to with the States-General in 1713; and this agreement was itself but a modification of the prior treaty of 1709, by which England had engaged to support the Dutch in obtaining a 'barrier' against France, consisting of a line of ten fortresses on the Flemish frontier. This treaty had been signed by Lord Townshend on behalf of England, as the Duke of Marlborough would have nothing to do with it. The agreement of 1713 had modified it considerably, to the disadvantage of the Dutch, and to the benefit commercially of England. The treaty had for one of its results strained relations between England and Austria prior to the outbreak of the Seven Years' War; and it was eventually annulled by the Treaty of Fontainebleau in 1785.

[2] This is an allusion to the rivalry between the Duchess of Marlborough and Mrs. Masham (who eventually supplanted her), which had been much inflamed when the latter had persuaded the Queen not to wear at the Thanksgiving Service for the victory of Oudenarde the jewels which the Duchess had arranged for her.

France and Spain; " Pam " is the Duke of Marlborough ; the Tea-Table is the Council ; the squabbling after the Rape represents the fierce political discussions ; Dapperwit is the President of the Council [Earl of Nottingham] ; the bodkin is the royal sceptre ; the three seal-rings are the three kingdoms ; and the happy ending is the Peace of Utrecht. Considered from the point of view of religion and the propagation of Popery, we may look upon the Sylphs as symbolizing the guardian angels and patron saints which figure so largely in Roman Catholicism ; the Toilette being the Mass, and the Chief Goddess our Lady of Loretto ; Belinda herself is the " Scarlet Woman ", and by the lunar sphere is typified Purgatory.'

It will be seen from this how very far-fetched and ridiculous is the matter of *the Key to the Lock*.

V

Numerous references have been made above to the ' machinery ' of the poem, which is a matter of interest from many points of view. Incidentally, the question of its intro-duction gave rise to the misunderstanding between Pope and Addison, to which we owe the celebrated portrait of 'Atticus' —a score of lines as unmatched in polished satire as they were, in all probability, unjust in fact. It is Pope's use of this machinery, moreover, which, more than any other single feature, made the poem the signal success that it is. Further-more, the whole subject of the Rosicrucian Fraternity is in itself a curious one. While it has made not a little noise in the world, its origin, character, and indeed its existence are only known from the claims of anonymous *ex parte* mani-festoes, such as the *Fama Fraternitatis*. Though it is now generally regarded as a mere hoax, at least one writer has seen in it a benevolent secret society, probably founded by Bacon, to which we owe not merely ' Shakespeare ', but the works of most of the leading Elizabethans.

It will be sufficient, however, for our present purpose to give some account of the work on which Pope's knowledge of the subject was mainly based.

The Spectator for May 15, 1712, the day after Pope's *Messiah* had appeared in that paper, had contained an account of the discovery of the Tomb of Rosicrucius. The article in question is usually attributed to Eustace Budgell, who was Addison's cousin and secretary ; and Dr. Johnson used to say that ' Addison wrote Budgell's papers in *The Spectator*, at least mended them so much that he made them almost his own.' It may have been this paper which first turned Pope's attention to the subject of the Rosicrucians, but whether that is so or not, he says in the Introductory Letter to Miss Fermor that the best account of them known to him is to be found ' in a French book called *Le Comte de Gabalis* '. This book was originally published in 1670, and the full title was *Le Comte de Gabalis ou Entretiens sur les sciences secrètes*. It was written by the Abbé de Montfaucon de Villars, though it has been asserted that it originated with one Joseph Francis Borri, a Milanese quack, who died in 1695. The Abbé, however, was looked upon as its author by his contemporaries ; for, although the book was well received at first, it soon came to be considered as dangerous and was proscribed, and the Abbé was forbidden to preach ; and three years after its publication he was assassinated on the road near Lyons. Pope's mention of this book in the Introductory Letter to *The Rape of the Lock* led to its being translated into English and published in London in the same year, 1714.

Prefixed to this English translation is Bayle's 'Account of the Rosicrucians', in which it is stated that the fraternity first appeared in Germany in the beginning of the seventeenth century, and that according to their own account the sect was founded by a 'Gentleman of Germany, whose name is not known but by these two letters, A. C.'; that this founder had died in 1484 after communicating to his disciples the secrets (including that of the Philosopher's Stone) which he had himself learned from the Arabs in Damascus. From the *Comte de Gabalis* Pope conceived the idea of elaborating *The Rape of the Lock* by the introduction of the 'machinery' of the Sylphs and Gnomes; which would have the effect of heightening the mock-heroic character of the poem, and at the same time render it more impersonal in tone, and so less distasteful to the Fermor family. Most of the friends to whom he communicated his idea seem to have warmly approved of it, and in particular Dr. Garth, who had himself written a mock-epic, *The Dispensary*, which does not, however, comprise any similar 'machinery'. The one dissentient was Addison, who urged Pope to leave the poem as it stood, saying that it was 'a delicious little thing' and 'merum sal' (pure wit). Pope, however, took umbrage at this attitude on Addison's part, and, as mentioned above, it led to an estrangement between them which was never entirely healed.

Pope himself was especially pleased and proud of the new production, and afterwards spoke of it as 'one of the greatest proofs of judgment of anything I ever did'. What he did was to convert a mere squib, too free and personal considering his want of acquaintance with the persons against whom it was directed, into a masterly and playful satire upon the follies and frivolities of the fashionable young ladies and beaux of

he day. At the same time he keeps in touch with Miss
Arabella, and while telling her that ' the character of Belinda,
as it is now managed, resembles you in nothing but beauty ',
he contrives, with wonderful tact, as a French critic has
pointed out, to let her see that she herself was not entirely
free from blame in the matter which had given rise to the
trouble.

Fully to appreciate the deftness with which Pope has
turned to account the *Comte de Gabalis*, we must consider
for a few moments what precisely is meant by ' machinery '
and its place in epic poetry. The meaning of the word, in
this connexion, is the interposition of some supernatural
agency or personage in a poem. Pope's own words, though
written in a spirit of banter, are very significant : ' The use
of these machines is evident : since no epic poem can possibly
subsist without them, the wisest way is to reserve them for
your greatest necessities : when you cannot extricate your
hero by any human means, or yourself by your own wit, seek
relief from heaven, and the gods will do your business very
readily ' (*The Art of Sinking in Poetry. For the machines*).
Similarly, Professor Ker, in his *Epic and Romance*, speaking
of the stories told to the Phaeacians in the *Odyssey*, says, 'The
episodes of Circe, of the Sirens, and of Polyphemus, are
machines.'

In the first half of the eighteenth century, all classes of
literature had a more or less conventional form, and consequently lent themselves to burlesque far more readily than
the literature of our own day. Gay's *Beggar's Opera* and
Swift's *Gulliver's Travels* are two instances which readily
suggest themselves, as being burlesques respectively of the
conventional methods of dramatists and of writers of travels.
As regards Epic poetry, the theory of Aristotle and the

practice of Homer and Virgil were supreme. Every poem
began with a stereotyped invocation of the Muse, it invariably
contained episodes, machinery, and all the rest of it, and
ended in a well-recognized fashion. The original version of
The Rape of the Lock was lacking in many characteristics which
a reader naturally looked for in an epic ; and Pope by the
introduction of ' machinery ', and especially of ' machinery '
derived from an unwonted source, made his poem far more
complete and mock-heroic. The spirits of the Rosicrucian
philosophy gave him exactly what he wanted. Instead of
the hackneyed gods and goddesses of Homer and Virgil, the
angels of Tasso, the personification of Discord, Faith, and so
on, of the *Lutrin* of Boileau, he found in *Le Comte de Gabalis*
his sylphs, gnomes, nymphs, and salamanders ready to his
hand. It is true that he found himself under the necessity
of altering in many particulars the account of these as given
in the French book, but that was easily done without
impairing the novelty of the thing ; and the grace and dex-
terity with which it was accomplished only added to the
charm of the poem.[1]

We must not leave the subject of the ' machinery ' without
calling attention to a remark recently made by Professor
Macaulay, who has ingeniously compared Pope with James
Thomson, his junior by twelve years. Thomson, he says,

---

[1] The sylphs, however, had not been entirely neglected by previous
French writers, for Madame de Sévigné makes mention of them as
invisible attendants upon ladies : and Horace Walpole added ' There
is nothing new under the sun ' to his note pointing out that Sonnerat
in his *Voyage aux Indes orientales* (1782), describes the ' Grandouvers '
of East Indian mythology in terms corresponding with Pope's sylphs.
Later on, we have the Glendoveer in Southey's *Curse of Kehama*,
borrowed from the same source ; and the *Undine* of de la Motte Fouqué
is but another name for ' nymph ' ; indeed the *Comte de Gabalis* speaks
of them as ' undines, or nymphs '.

was ' in a certain sense the complement of Pope, applying to country scenes something of the same power of true observation and vivid portraiture which Pope used upon the town ' ; and he goes on to point out that the introduction by Pope of the machinery of the sylphs to ' embroider ' his description of town life in *The Rape of the Lock* is analogous to the use made by Thomson of man's relations with nature.

VI

We have referred above to the *Lutrin* of Boileau, which is one of the instances usually adduced of mock-heroic poems prior in point of date to *The Rape of the Lock*. This had appeared in 1674, and was undoubtedly the best production of the kind until it was excelled by Pope. It records, in a comic epic fashion, the petty squabbles of the chapter of La Sainte Chapelle in Paris over the position of a lectern. Another predecessor, written just 100 years before *The Rape of the Lock*, was the *Secchia Rapita* (Rape of the Bucket) of Alessandro Tassoni, which describes in comic fashion the battles of the Bolognese and Sardinians in 1249. Tassoni himself claims to have been the first to combine the heroic, the comic, and the satiric in one poem (Muratori, *Vita di Tassoni*, p. 81) ; but, as far as the heroic and the comic are concerned, he had to some extent been anticipated both by the *Morgante Maggiore* of Pulci and the *Orlando Furioso* of Ariosto. Garth's *Dispensary*, of which we have already made mention, was also prior in point of date to *The Rape of the Lock*, but there is not much that is ' comic ' in it, and it can scarcely be regarded as a serious competitor. Of course there are instances among the classics of the ironical treat-ment of trifling subjects as if they were matters of great importance, notably *The Battle of the Frogs and Mice*, attributed to Homer, but they may be left out of account as being of too old a date to come into comparison.

Another addition which, although of minor importance compared with the introduction of the Rosicrucian sylphs furnishes one of the most brilliant episodes of the poem— the game of Ombre (as to which see Appendix, p. 93)—was suggested to Pope by the *Scacchia Ludus* (Game of Chess) of Vida. Vida, who was Bishop of Alba, died in 1566, and the poem, an admirable description of a game of chess in Latin hexameters, was published at Rome in 1527. It is interesting to note that, when Pope came in after years (1740) to edit two little volumes of *Selecta Poemata Italorum*, his selections from Vida included the *Scacchia Ludus*; and that Goldsmith left an English translation at his death in 1774.

We shall not attempt to follow out the well-known story of Pope's life subsequent to the publication of *The Rape of the Lock*. To do so with any detail would take up far more space than we have at our present disposal; but a short chronological table has been appended which may be useful for reference. As a last word, we may point out that it is, to say the least, interesting to find that the play of Menander (Περικειρομένη = *Circumtonsa*) which has at last been brought to light among the Oxyrhynchus papyri, has for its subject the cutting off of a lady's hair.

G. H.

CHRONOLOGICAL TABLE OF POPE'S PRINCIPAL
PUBLICATIONS, AND SOME OF THE CHIEF
EVENTS IN HIS LIFE, SUBSEQUENT TO 1713.

1714 *Prologue to Addison's Cato. Windsor Forest.* His breach with
Addison—joins the 'Scriblerus Club' (Swift, Arbuthnot, Congreve, &c.). Takes lessons in painting from Charles Jervas.
Translation of the Iliad projected.

1715 First book of the *Iliad* published.

1716 The Pope family moved from Binfield to Chiswick.

1717 Pope's father died. *Eloisa to Abelard.*

1718 Fifth volume of the *Iliad* finished at Stanton Harcourt. Lady
Mary Wortley Montagu returned from the East.

1719 Pope bought lease of house and five acres of land at Twickenham.
Lady M. W. Montagu came and lived near him. He invested
in the South Sea Stock. Addison died.

1722 Quarrelled with Lady M. W. Montagu. Edited Parnell's poems.
Began his edition of Shakespeare.

1723 Atterbury exiled. Bolingbroke returned.

1725 Shakespeare a failure. First three volumes of his *Odyssey* published.
His nurse, Mary Beach, died. Bolingbroke settled at Dawley
near Twickenham.

1726 Swift visited him at Twickenham, and Pope arranged for him the
publication of *Gulliver's Travels.*

1727 Swift again visited him. *The Dunciad. Miscellanies.*

1728 *The Dunciad* published anonymously.

1729 Enlarged edition of *The Dunciad* published, with the names no
longer concealed under initials.

1732 Gay died.

1733 Pope's mother died. *Essay on Man.*

1735 *Epistle to Arbuthnot.* Arbuthnot died.

1736 John Caryll died. Bolingbroke returned to France.

1737 Pope's *Correspondence* published, as the result of intriguing and
very unworthy manœuvres on his part. His correspondence with
Swift published in similar fashion. *The Epistle to Augustus.*

1738 The *Epilogue to the Satires.* The *Universal Prayer.*

1740 Made the acquaintance of Warburton.

1741 Visited Oxford. Declined the honorary degree of D.C.L. Visited
   Ralph Allen at Prior Park, near Bath.

1742 Fourth book of *The Dunciad*, with Cibber substituted for Theobald
   as the hero.

1743 Bolingbroke returned to England.

1744 Quarrelled with Ralph Allen at the instigation of Martha Blount.
   His death on May 30. Buried at Twickenham on June 5.

1761 Warburton erected a monument in Twickenham Church ' to one
   who would not be buried in Westminster Abbey '.

The Standard Edition of Pope's Works is that in ten volumes, published by Murray in 1871–89 : it is the joint work of the Rev. Whitwell
Elwin and Mr. W. J. Courthope.

THE RAPE OF THE LOCK
AN HEROI-COMICAL POEM

TO MRS. ARABELLA FERMOR

MADAM,

IT will be in vain to deny that I have some regard for this piece, since I dedicate it to you. Yet you may bear me witness, it was intended only to divert a few young ladies, who have good sense and good humour enough to laugh not only at their sex's little unguarded follies, but at their own. But as it was communicated with the air of a Secret, it soon found its way into the world. An imperfect copy having been offer'd to a Bookseller, you had the good-nature for my sake to consent to the publication of one more correct : This I was forced to, before I had executed half my design, for the Machinery was entirely wanting to complete it.

The Machinery, Madam, is a term invented by the Critics, to signify that part which the Deities, Angels, or Demons are made to act in a Poem : For the ancient Poets are in one respect like many modern Ladies : let an action be never so trivial in itself, they always make it appear of the utmost importance. These Machines I determined to raise on a very new and odd foundation, the Rosicrucian doctrine of Spirits.

I know how disagreeable it is to make use of hard words before a Lady ; but 'tis so much the concern of a Poet to have his works understood, and particularly by your Sex, that you must give me leave to explain two or three difficult terms.

The Rosicrucians are a people I must bring you acquainted with. The best account I know of them is in a French book call'd *Le Comte de Gabalis*, which both in its title and size is so like a Novel, that many of the Fair Sex have read it for one by mistake. According to these Gentlemen, the four Elements are inhabited by Spirits, which they call Sylphs, Gnomes, Nymphs, and Salamanders. The Gnomes or Demons of Earth delight in mischief : but the Sylphs, whose habitation is in the Air, are the best-condition'd Creatures imaginable. For they say, any mortals may enjoy the most intimate familiarities with these gentle Spirits, upon a condition very easy to all true Adepts, an inviolate preservation of Chastity.

As to the following Cantos, all the passages of them are as fabulous, as the Vision at the beginning, or the Transformation at the end ; (except the loss of your Hair, which I always mention with reverence).   The Human persons are as fictitious as the Airy ones ; and the Character of Belinda, as it is now manag'd, resembles you in nothing but in Beauty.

If this Poem had as many Graces as there are in your Person, or in your Mind, yet I could never hope it should pass through the world half so Uncensur'd as You have done.   But let its fortune be what it will, mine is happy enough, to have given me this occasion of assuring you that I am, with the truest esteem, MADAM,

Your most obedient, humble servant,
A. POPE.

Nolueram, Belinda, tuos violare capillos ;
　　Sed iuvat hoc precibus me tribuisse tuis.—MARTIAL.

CANTO I

WHAT dire offence from amorous causes springs,
What mighty contests rise from trivial things,
I sing—This verse to CARYL, Muse ! is due :
This, even Belinda may vouchsafe to view :
Slight is the subject, but not so the praise,　　　　　　5
If she inspire, and he approve my lays.

　Say what strange motive, Goddess ! could compel
A well-bred lord to assault a gentle belle?
O say what stranger cause, yet unexplored,
Could make a gentle belle reject a lord?　　　　　　10
In tasks so bold, can little men engage,
And in soft bosoms dwells such mighty rage?

　Sol through white curtains shot a timorous ray,
And oped those eyes that must eclipse the day :
Now lap-dogs give themselves the rousing shake,　　　15
And sleepless lovers, just at twelve, awake :
Thrice rung the bell, the slipper knocked the ground,
And the pressed watch returned a silver sound.
Belinda still her downy pillow pressed,
Her guardian sylph prolonged the balmy rest :　　　　20
'Twas he had summoned to her silent bed
The morning-dream that hovered o'er her head ;
A youth more glittering than a birth-night beau,
(That even in slumber caused her cheek to glow)
Seemed to her ear his winning lips to lay,　　　　　　25
And thus in whispers said, or seemed to say.

　' Fairest of mortals, thou distinguished care
Of thousand bright inhabitants of air !

If e'er one vision touched thy infant thought,
Of all the nurse and all the priest have taught;   30
Of airy elves by moonlight shadows seen,
The silver token, and the circled green,
Or virgins visited by angel-powers,
With golden crowns and wreaths of heavenly flowers;
Hear and believe! thy own importance know,   35
Nor bound thy narrow views to things below.
Some secret truths, from learned pride concealed,
To maids alone and children are revealed:
What though no credit doubting wits may give!
The fair and innocent shall still believe.   40
Know, then, unnumbered spirits round thee fly,
The light militia of the lower sky:
These, though unseen, are ever on the wing,
Hang o'er the box, and hover round the ring.
Think what an equipage thou hast in air,   45
And view with scorn two pages and a chair.
As now your own, our beings were of old,
And once inclosed in woman's beauteous mould;
Thence, by a soft transition, we repair
From earthly vehicles to these of air.   50
Think not, when woman's transient breath is fled,
That all her vanities at once are dead;
Succeeding vanities she still regards,
And though she plays no more, o'erlooks the cards.
Her joy in gilded chariots, when alive,   55
And love of ombre, after death survive.
For when the fair in all their pride expire,
To their first elements their souls retire:
The sprites of fiery termagants in flame
Mount up, and take a salamander's name.   60

Soft yielding minds to water glide away,
And sip, with nymphs, their elemental tea.
The graver prude sinks downward to a gnome,
In search of mischief still on earth to roam.
The light coquettes in sylphs aloft repair, 65
And sport and flutter in the fields of air.
  ' Know further yet ; whoever fair and chaste
Rejects mankind, is by some sylph embraced :
For spirits, freed from mortal laws, with ease
Assume what sexes and what shapes they please. 70
What guards the purity of melting maids,
In courtly balls, and midnight masquerades,
Safe from the treacherous friend, the daring spark,
The glance by day, the whisper in the dark,
When kind occasion prompts their warm desires, 75
When music softens, and when dancing fires?
'Tis but their sylph, the wise celestials know,
Though honour is the word with men below.
  ' Some nymphs there are, too conscious of their face,
For life predestined to the gnomes' embrace. 80
These swell their prospects and exalt their pride,
When offers are disdained, and love denied :
Then gay ideas crowd the vacant brain,
While peers, and dukes, and all their sweeping train,
And garters, stars, and coronets appear, 85
And in soft sounds, " Your Grace " salutes their ear.
'Tis these that early taint the female soul,
Instruct the eyes of young coquettes to roll,
Teach infant-cheeks a bidden blush to know,
And little hearts to flutter at a beau. 90
  ' Oft, when the world imagine women stray,
The sylphs through mystic mazes guide their way,

Through all the giddy circle they pursue,
And old impertinence expel by new.
What tender maid but must a victim fall   95
To one man's treat, but for another's ball?
When Florio speaks, what virgin could withstand,
If gentle Damon did not squeeze her hand?
With varying vanities, from every part,
They shift the moving toyshop of their heart;   100
Where wigs with wigs, with sword-knots sword-knots strive,
Beaux banish beaux, and coaches coaches drive.
This erring mortals levity may call;
Oh blind to truth! the sylphs contrive it all.

'Of these am I, who thy protection claim,   105
A watchful sprite, and Ariel is my name.
Late, as I ranged the crystal wilds of air,
In the clear mirror of thy ruling star
I saw, alas! some dread event impend,
Ere to the main this morning sun descend,   110
But heaven reveals not what, or how, or where:
Warned by the sylph, oh pious maid, beware!
This to disclose is all thy guardian can:
Beware of all, but most beware of man!'

He said; when Shock, who thought she slept too long, 115
Leaped up, and waked his mistress with his tongue.
'Twas then, Belinda, if report say true,
Thy eyes first opened on a billet-doux;
Wounds, charms, and ardours were no sooner read,
But all the vision vanished from thy head.   120

And now, unveiled, the toilet stands displayed,
Each silver vase in mystic order laid.
First, robed in white, the nymph intent adores,
With head uncovered, the cosmetic powers.

A heavenly image in the glass appears, 125
To that she bends, to that her eyes she rears;
The inferior priestess, at her altar's side,
Trembling begins the sacred rites of pride.
Unnumbered treasures ope at once, and here
The various offerings of the world appear; 130
From each she nicely culls with curious toil,
And decks the Goddess with the glittering spoil.
This casket India's glowing gems unlocks,
And all Arabia breathes from yonder box.
The tortoise here and elephant unite, 135
Transformed to combs, the speckled, and the white.
Here files of pins extend their shining rows,
Puffs, powders, patches, bibles, billet-doux.
Now awful beauty puts on all its arms;
The fair each moment rises in her charms, 140
Repairs her smiles, awakens every grace,
And calls forth all the wonders of her face;
Sees by degrees a purer blush arise,
And keener lightnings quicken in her eyes.
The busy sylphs surround their darling care, 145
These set the head, and those divide the hair,
Some fold the sleeve, whilst others plait the gown;
And Betty's praised for labours not her own.

CANTO II

Not with more glories, in the ethereal plain,
The sun first rises o'er the purpled main,
Than, issuing forth, the rival of his beams
Launched on the bosom of the silver Thames.

Fair nymphs, and well-dressed youths around her shone, 5
But every eye was fixed on her alone.
On her white breast a sparkling cross she wore,
Which Jews might kiss, and infidels adore.
Her lively looks a sprightly mind disclose,
Quick as her eyes, and as unfixed as those : 10
Favours to none, to all she smiles extends ;
Oft she rejects, but never once offends.
Bright as the sun, her eyes the gazers strike,
And, like the sun, they shine on all alike.
Yet graceful ease, and sweetness void of pride, 15
Might hide her faults, if belles had faults to hide :
If to her share some female errors fall,
Look on her face, and you'll forget 'em all.

This nymph, to the destruction of mankind,
Nourished two locks, which graceful hung behind 20
In equal curls, and well conspired to deck
With shining ringlets the smooth iv'ry neck.
Love in these labyrinths his slaves detains,
And mighty hearts are held in slender chains.
With hairy springes we the birds betray, 25
Slight lines of hair surprise the finny prey,
Fair tresses man's imperial race ensnare,
And beauty draws us with a single hair.

The adventurous Baron the bright locks admired ;
He saw, he wished, and to the prize aspired. 30
Resolved to win, he meditates the way,
By force to ravish, or by fraud betray ;
For when success a lover's toil attends,
Few ask, if fraud or force attained his ends.

For this, ere Phoebus rose, he had implored 35
Propitious heaven, and every power adored,

But chiefly Love—to Love an altar built,
Of twelve vast French romances, neatly gilt.
There lay three garters, half a pair of gloves;
And all the trophies of his former loves;   40
With tender billet-doux he lights the pyre,
And breathes three amorous sighs to raise the fire.
Then prostrate falls, and begs with ardent eyes
Soon to obtain, and long possess the prize:
The powers gave ear, and granted half his prayer,   45
The rest the winds dispersed in empty air.
    But now secure the painted vessel glides,
The sun-beams trembling on the floating tides:
While melting music steals upon the sky,
And softened sounds along the waters die;   50
Smooth flow the waves, the zephyrs gently play,
Belinda smiled, and all the world was gay.
All but the sylph—with careful thoughts oppressed,
The impending woe sat heavy on his breast.
He summons straight his denizens of air;   55
The lucid squadrons round the sails repair:
Soft o'er the shrouds aërial whispers breathe,
That seemed but zephyrs to the train beneath.
Some to the sun their insect-wings unfold,
Waft on the breeze, or sink in clouds of gold;   60
Transparent forms, too fine for mortal sight,
Their fluid bodies half dissolved in light,
Loose to the wind their airy garments flew,
Thin glittering textures of the filmy dew,
Dipt in the richest tincture of the skies,   65
Where light disports in ever-mingling dyes,
While every beam new transient colours flings,
Colours that change whene'er they wave their wings.

Amid the circle, on the gilded mast,
Superior by the head, was Ariel placed;   70
His purple pinions opening to the sun,
He raised his azure wand, and thus begun.

   Ye sylphs and sylphids, to your chief give ear!
Fays, fairies, genii, elves, and demons, hear!
Ye know the spheres and various tasks assigned   75
By laws eternal to the aërial kind.
Some in the fields of purest ether play,
And bask and whiten in the blaze of day.
Some guide the course of wandering orbs on high,
Or roll the planets through the boundless sky.   80
Some less refined, beneath the moon's pale light
Pursue the stars that shoot athwart the night,
Or suck the mists in grosser air below,
Or dip their pinions in the painted bow,
Or brew fierce tempests on the wintry main,   85
Or o'er the glebe distil the kindly rain.
Others on earth o'er human race preside,
Watch all their ways, and all their actions guide:
Of these the chief the care of nations own,
And guard with arms divine the British throne.   90

   Our humbler province is to tend the fair,
Not a less pleasing, though less glorious care;
To save the powder from too rude a gale,
Nor let the imprisoned essences exhale;
To draw fresh colours from the vernal flowers;   95
To steal from rainbows ere they drop in showers
A brighter wash; to curl their waving hairs,
Assist their blushes, and inspire their airs;
Nay oft, in dreams, invention we bestow,
To change a flounce, or add a furbelow.   100

This day, black omens threat the brightest fair,
That e'er deserved a watchful spirit's care;
Some dire disaster, or by force, or slight;
But what, or where, the fates have wrapt in night.
Whether the nymph shall break Diana's law,   105
Or some frail china jar receive a flaw;
Or stain her honour or her new brocade;
Forget her prayers, or miss a masquerade;
Or lose her heart, or necklace, at a ball;
Or whether Heaven has doom'd that Shock must fall.   110
Haste, then, ye spirits! to your charge repair:
The fluttering fan be Zephyretta's care;
The drops to thee, Brillante, we consign;
And, Momentilla, let the watch be thine;
Do thou, Crispissa, tend her favourite lock;   115
Ariel himself shall be the guard of Shock.
    To fifty chosen sylphs, of special note,
We trust th' important charge, the petticoat:
Oft have we known that seven-fold fence to fail,
Though stiff with hoops, and armed with ribs of whale;   120
Form a strong line about the silver bound,
And guard the wide circumference around.
    Whatever spirit, careless of his charge,
His post neglects, or leaves the fair at large,
Shall feel sharp vengeance soon o'ertake his sins,   125
Be stopped in vials, or transfixed with pins;
Or plunged in lakes of bitter washes lie,
Or wedged whole ages in a bodkin's eye:
Gums and pomatums shall his flight restrain,
While clogged he beats his silken wings in vain;   130
Or alum styptics with contracting power
Shrink his thin essence like a rivelled flower:

Or, as Ixion fixed, the wretch shall feel
The giddy motion of the whirling mill,
In fumes of burning chocolate shall glow,   135
And tremble at the sea that froths below!

　He spoke; the spirits from the sails descend;
Some, orb in orb, around the nymph extend;
Some thrid the mazy ringlets of her hair;
Some hang upon the pendants of her ear: 140
With beating hearts the dire event they wait,
Anxious, and trembling for the birth of Fate.

CANTO III

Close by those meads, for ever crowned with flowers,
Where Thames with pride surveys his rising towers,
There stands a structure of majestic frame,
Which from the neighb'ring Hampton takes its name.
Here Britain's statesmen oft the fall foredoom   5
Of foreign tyrants and of nymphs at home;
Here thou, great Anna! whom three realms obey,
Dost sometimes counsel take—and sometimes tea.
　Hither the heroes and the nymphs resort,
To taste awhile the pleasures of a court;   10
In various talk the instructive hours they passed,
Who gave the ball, or paid the visit last;
One speaks the glory of the British queen,
And one describes a charming Indian screen;
A third interprets motions, looks, and eyes;   15
At every word a reputation dies.
Snuff, or the fan, supply each pause of chat,
With singing, laughing, ogling, and all that.

Meanwhile, declining from the noon of day,
The sun obliquely shoots his burning ray ; 20
The hungry judges soon the sentence sign,
And wretches hang that jury-men may dine ;
The merchant from the Exchange returns in peace,
And the long labours of the toilet cease.
Belinda now, whom thirst of fame invites, 25
Burns to encounter two adventurous knights,
At ombre singly to decide their doom ;
And swells her breast with conquests yet to come.
Straight the three bands prepare in arms to join,
Each band the number of the sacred nine. 30
Soon as she spreads her hand, the aërial guard
Descend, and sit on each important card :
First Ariel perched upon a Matadore,
Then each, according to the rank they bore ;
For sylphs, yet mindful of their ancient race, 35
Are, as when women, wondrous fond of place.
   Behold, four kings in majesty revered,
With hoary whiskers and a forky beard ;
And four fair queens whose hands sustain a flower,
The expressive emblem of their softer power ; 40
Four knaves in garbs succinct, a trusty band,
Caps on their heads, and halberts in their hand ;
And parti-coloured troops, a shining train,
Draw forth to combat on the velvet plain.
   The skilful nymph reviews her force with care : 45
Let spades be trumps ! she said, and trumps they were
   Now move to war her sable Matadores,
In show like leaders of the swarthy Moors.
Spadillio first, unconquerable lord !
Led off two captive trumps, and swept the board. 50

As many more Manillio forced to yield,
And marched a victor from the verdant field.
Him Basto followed, but his fate more hard
Gained but one trump and one plebeian card.
With his broad sabre next, a chief in years,   55
The hoary majesty of spades appears,
Puts forth one manly leg, to sight revealed,
The rest, his many-coloured robe concealed.
The rebel knave, who dares his prince engage,
Proves the just victim of his royal rage.   60
Even mighty Pam, that kings and queens o'erthrew,
And mowed down armies in the fights of Lu,
Sad chance of war! now destitute of aid,
Falls undistinguished by the victor spade!

Thus far both armies to Belinda yield;   65
Now to the Baron fate inclines the field.
His warlike Amazon her host invades,
The imperial consort of the crown of spades.
The club's black tyrant first her victim died,
Spite of his haughty mien, and barbarous pride: 70
What boots the regal circle on his head,
His giant limbs, in state unwieldy spread;
That long behind he trails his pompous robe,
And, of all monarchs, only grasps the globe?
The Baron now his diamonds pours apace;   75
The embroidered king who shows but half his face,
And his refulgent queen, with powers combined,
Of broken troops an easy conquest find.
Clubs, diamonds, hearts, in wild disorder seen,
With throngs promiscuous strow the level green.   80
Thus when dispersed a routed army runs,
Of Asia's troops, and Afric's sable sons,

With like confusion different nations fly,
Of various habit, and of various dye,
The pierced battalions disunited fall,   85
In heaps on heaps; one fate o'erwhelms them all.
  The knave of diamonds tries his wily arts,
And wins (oh shameful chance!) the queen of hearts.
At this, the blood the virgin's cheek forsook,
A livid paleness spreads o'er all her look;   90
She sees, and trembles at the approaching ill,
Just in the jaws of ruin, and codille.
And now (as oft in some distempered state)
On one nice trick depends the general fate:
An ace of hearts steps forth: the king unseen   95
Lurked in her hand, and mourned his captive queen:
He springs to vengeance with an eager pace,
And falls like thunder on the prostrate ace.
The nymph exulting fills with shouts the sky;
The walls, the woods, and long canals reply.   100
  O thoughtless mortals! ever blind to fate,
Too soon dejected, and too soon elate.
Sudden, these honours shall be snatched away,
And cursed for ever this victorious day.
  For lo! the board with cups and spoons is crowned,   105
The berries crackle, and the mill turns round;
On shining altars of Japan they raise
The silver lamp; the fiery spirits blaze:
From silver spouts the grateful liquors glide,
While China's earth receives the smoking tide: 110
At once they gratify their scent and taste,
And frequent cups prolong the rich repast.
Straight hover round the fair her airy band;
Some, as she sipped, the fuming liquor fanned,

Some o'er her lap their careful plumes displayed, 115
Trembling, and conscious of the rich brocade.
Coffee, (which makes the politician wise,
And see through all things with his half-shut eyes)
Sent up in vapours to the Baron's brain
New stratagems, the radiant lock to gain. 120
Ah cease, rash youth! desist ere 'tis too late,
Fear the just Gods, and think of Scylla's fate!
Changed to a bird, and sent to flit in air,
She dearly pays for Nisus' injured hair!

But when to mischief mortals bend their will, 125
How soon they find fit instruments of ill!
Just then, Clarissa drew with tempting grace
A two-edged weapon from her shining case:
So ladies in romance assist their knight,
Present the spear, and arm him for the fight. 130
He takes the gift with reverence, and extends
The little engine on his fingers' ends;
This just behind Belinda's neck he spread,
As o'er the fragrant steams she bends her head.
Swift to the lock a thousand sprites repair, 135
A thousand wings, by turns, blow back the hair;
And thrice they twitched the diamond in her ear;
Thrice she looked back, and thrice the foe drew near.
Just in that instant, anxious Ariel sought
The close recesses of the virgin's thought; 140
As on the nosegay in her breast reclined,
He watched the ideas rising in her mind,
Sudden he viewed, in spite of all her art,
An earthly lover lurking at her heart.
Amazed, confused, he found his power expired, 145
Resigned to fate, and with a sigh retired.

The peer now spreads the glittering forfex wide,
To inclose the lock; now joins it, to divide.
Even then, before the fatal engine closed,
A wretched sylph too fondly interposed;   150
Fate urged the shears, and cut the sylph in twain,
(But airy substance soon unites again)
The meeting points the sacred hair dissever
From the fair head, for ever, and for ever!

   Then flashed the living lightning from her eyes,   155
And screams of horror rend the affrighted skies.
Not louder shrieks to pitying heaven are cast,
When husbands, or when lap-dogs breathe their last;
Or when rich China vessels fallen from high,
In glittering dust and painted fragments lie!   160

   Let wreaths of triumph now my temples twine,
(The victor cried) the glorious prize is mine!
While fish in streams, or birds delight in air,
Or in a coach and six the British fair,
As long as Atalantis shall be read,   165
Or the small pillow grace a lady's bed,
While visits shall be paid on solemn days,
When numerous wax-lights in bright order blaze,
While nymphs take treats, or assignations give,
So long my honour, name, and praise shall live!   170
What time would spare, from steel receives its date,
And monuments, like men, submit to fate!
Steel could the labour of the Gods destroy,
And strike to dust the imperial towers of Troy;
Steel could the works of mortal pride confound,   175
And hew triumphal arches to the ground.
What wonder then, fair nymph! thy hairs should feel
The conquering force of unresisted steel?

CANTO IV

But anxious cares the pensive nymph oppressed,
And secret passions laboured in her breast.
Not youthful kings in battle seized alive,
Not scornful virgins who their charms survive,
Not ardent lovers robbed of all their bliss,   5
Not ancient ladies when refused a kiss,
Not tyrants fierce that unrepenting die,
Not Cynthia when her manteau's pinned awry,
E'er felt such rage, resentment, and despair,
As thou, sad virgin! for thy ravished hair.   10

For, that sad moment, when the sylphs withdrew
And Ariel weeping from Belinda flew,
Umbriel, a dusky, melancholy sprite,
As ever sullied the fair face of light,
Down to the central earth, his proper scene,   15
Repaired to search the gloomy Cave of Spleen.

Swift on his sooty pinions flits the gnome,
And in a vapour reached the dismal dome.
No cheerful breeze this sullen region knows,
The dreaded east is all the wind that blows.   20
Here in a grotto, sheltered close from air,
And screened in shades from day's detested glare,
She sighs for ever on her pensive bed,
Pain at her side, and Megrim at her head.

Two handmaids wait the throne: alike in place,   25
But differing far in figure and in face.
Here stood Ill-nature like an ancient maid,
Her wrinkled form in black and white arrayed;
With store of prayers, for mornings, nights, and noons,
Her hand is filled; her bosom with lampoons.   30

There Affection, with a sickly mien,
Shows in her cheek the roses of eighteen,
Practised to lisp, and hang the head aside,
Faints into airs, and languishes with pride,
On the rich quilt sinks with becoming woe,   35
Wrapt in a gown, for sickness, and for show.
The fair ones feel such maladies as these,
When each new night-dress gives a new disease.

A constant vapour o'er the palace flies;
Strange phantoms rising as the mists arise;   40
Dreadful, as hermit's dreams in haunted shades,
Or bright, as visions of expiring maids.
Now glaring fiends, and snakes on rolling spires,
Pale spectres, gaping tombs, and purple fires:
Now lakes of liquid gold, Elysian scenes,   45
And crystal domes, and angels in machines.

Unnumbered throngs on every side are seen,
Of bodies changed to various forms by Spleen.
Here living tea-pots stand, one arm held out,
One bent; the handle this, and that the spout: 50
A pipkin there, like Homer's tripod, walks;
Here sighs a jar, and there a goose-pye talks;
Men prove with child, as powerful fancy works,
And maids turned bottles, call aloud for corks.

Safe passed the gnome through this fantastic band,   55
A branch of healing spleenwort in his hand.
Then thus address'd the power: 'Hail, wayward Queen!
Who rule the sex to fifty from fifteen:
Parent of vapours and of female wit,
Who give the hysteric, or poetic fit,   60
On various tempers act by various ways,
Make some take physic, others scribble plays;

Who cause the proud their visits to delay,
And send the godly in a pet to pray.
A nymph there is, that all thy power disdains,　　6
And thousands more in equal mirth maintains.
But oh! if e'er thy gnome could spoil a grace,
Or raise a pimple on a beauteous face,
Like citron-waters matrons' cheeks inflame,
Or change complexions at a losing game;　　7
If e'er with airy horns I planted heads,
Or rumpled petticoats, or tumbled beds,
Or caused suspicion when no soul was rude,
Or discomposed the head-dress of a prude,
Or e'er to costive lap-dog gave disease,　　7
Which not the tears of brightest eyes could ease:
Hear me, and touch Belinda with chagrin,
That single act gives half the world the spleen.'
　　The Goddess with a discontented air
Seems to reject him, though she grants his prayer.　　8
A wondrous bag with both her hands she binds,
Like that where once Ulysses held the winds;
There she collects the force of female lungs,
Sighs, sobs, and passions, and the war of tongues.
A vial next she fills with fainting fears,　　8
Soft sorrows, melting griefs, and flowing tears.
The gnome rejoicing bears her gifts away,
Spreads his black wings, and slowly mounts to day.
　　Sunk in Thalestris' arms the nymph he found,
Her eyes dejected and her hair unbound.　　9
Full o'er their heads the swelling bag he rent,
And all the Furies issued at the vent.
Belinda burns with more than mortal ire,
And fierce Thalestris fans the rising fire.

O wretched maid!' she spread her hands, and cried, 95
While Hampton's echoes, 'Wretched maid!' replied)
Was it for this you took such constant care
The bodkin, comb, and essence to prepare?
For this your locks in paper durance bound,
For this with torturing irons wreathed around? 100
For this with fillets strained your tender head,
And bravely bore the double loads of lead?
Gods! shall the ravisher display your hair,
While the fops envy, and the ladies stare!
Honour forbid! at whose unrivalled shrine 105
Ease, pleasure, virtue, all, our sex resign.
Methinks already I your tears survey,
Already hear the horrid things they say,
Already see you a degraded toast,
And all your honour in a whisper lost! 110
How shall I, then, your hapless fame defend?
'Twill then be infamy to seem your friend!
And shall this prize, the inestimable prize,
Exposed through crystal to the gazing eyes,
And heightened by the diamond's circling rays, 115
On that rapacious hand for ever blaze?
Sooner shall grass in Hyde-park Circus grow,
And wits take lodgings in the sound of Bow;
Sooner let earth, air, sea, to chaos fall,
Men, monkeys, lap-dogs, parrots, perish all!' 120
    She said; then raging to Sir Plume repairs,
And bids her beau demand the precious hairs:
Sir Plume of amber snuff-box justly vain,
And the nice conduct of a clouded cane)
With earnest eyes, and round unthinking face, 125
He first the snuff-box opened, then the case,

And thus broke out—'My Lord, why, what the devil?
Zounds! damn the lock! 'fore Gad, you must be civil
Plague on't! 'tis past a jest—nay prithee, pox!
Give her the hair'—he spoke, and rapp'd his box   130
  'It grieves me much' (replied the Peer again)
'Who speaks so well should ever speak in vain.
But by this lock, this sacred lock I swear,
(Which never more shall join its parted hair;
Which never more its honours shall renew,   135
Clipped from the lovely head where late it grew)
That while my nostrils draw the vital air,
This hand, which won it, shall for ever wear.
He spoke, and speaking, in proud triumph spread
The long-contended honours of her head.   140
  But Umbriel, hateful gnome! forbears not so;
He breaks the vial whence the sorrows flow.
Then see! the nymph in beauteous grief appears,
Her eyes half-languishing, half-drowned in tears;
On her heaved bosom hung her drooping head,   145
Which, with a sigh, she raised; and thus she said.
  'For ever cursed be this detested day,
Which snatched my best, my favourite curl away!
Happy! ah ten times happy had I been,
If Hampton-Court these eyes had never seen!   150
Yet am not I the first mistaken maid,
By love of courts to numerous ills betrayed.
Oh had I rather un-admired remained
In some lone isle, or distant northern land;
Where the gilt chariot never marks the way,   155
Where none learn ombre, none e'er taste bohea!
There kept my charms concealed from mortal eye,
Like roses, that in deserts bloom and die.

What moved my mind with youthful lords to roam?
Oh had I stayed, and said my prayers at home! 160
'Twas this, the morning omens seemed to tell,
Thrice from my trembling hand the patch-box fell;
The tottering China shook without a wind,
Nay, Poll sat mute, and Shock was most unkind!
A sylph too warned me of the threats of fate, 165
In mystic visions, now believed too late!
See the poor remnants of these slighted hairs!
My hands shall rend what ev'n thy rapine spares:
These in two sable ringlets taught to break,
Once gave new beauties to the snowy neck; 170
The sister-lock now sits uncouth, alone,
And in its fellow's fate foresees its own;
Uncurled it hangs, the fatal shears demands,
And tempts once more thy sacrilegious hands.
Oh hadst thou, cruel! been content to seize 175
Hairs less in sight, or any hairs but these!'

CANTO V

SHE said: the pitying audience melt in tears,
But fate and Jove had stopped the Baron's ears.
In vain Thalestris with reproach assails,
For who can move when fair Belinda fails?
Not half so fixed the Trojan could remain, 5
While Anna begged and Dido raged in vain.
Then grave Clarissa graceful waved her fan;
Silence ensued, and thus the nymph began.
  'Say, why are beauties praised and honoured most,
The wise man's passion, and the vain man's toast? 10

I

Why decked with all that land and sea afford,
Why Angels called, and Angel-like adored?
Why round our coaches crowd the white-gloved beaux,
Why bows the side-box from its inmost rows?
How vain are all these glories, all our pains,   15
Unless good sense preserve what beauty gains :
That men may say, when we the front-box grace :
" Behold the first in virtue as in face ! "
Oh! if to dance all night, and dress all day,
Charmed the small-pox, or chased old-age away ;   20
Who would not scorn what housewife's cares produce,
Or who would learn one earthly thing of use?
To patch, nay ogle, might become a saint,
Nor could it sure be such a sin to paint.
But since, alas ! frail beauty must decay,   25
Curled or uncurled, since locks will turn to grey ;
Since painted, or not painted, all shall fade,
And she who scorns a man, must die a maid ;
What then remains but well our power to use,
And keep good-humour still whate'er we lose?   30
And trust me, dear ! good-humour can prevail,
When airs, and flights, and screams, and scolding fail.
Beauties in vain their pretty eyes may roll ;
Charms strike the sight, but merit wins the soul.'

So spoke the dame, but no applause ensued ;   35
Belinda frowned, Thalestris called her prude.
' To arms, to arms ! ' the fierce virago cries,
And swift as lightning to the combat flies.
All side in parties, and begin the attack ;
Fans clap, silks rustle, and tough whalebones crack ;   40
Heroes' and heroines' shouts confusedly rise,
And base and treble voices strike the skies.

No common weapons in their hands are found,
Like gods they fight, nor dread a mortal wound.
  So when bold Homer makes the gods engage,   45
And heavenly breasts with human passions rage ;
'Gainst Pallas, Mars ; Latona, Hermes arms ;
And all Olympus rings with loud alarms :
Jove's thunder roars, heaven trembles all around,
Blue Neptune storms, the bellowing deeps resound :   50
Earth shakes her nodding towers, the ground gives way,
And the pale ghosts start at the flash of day !
  Triumphant Umbriel on a sconce's height
Clapped his glad wings, and sate to view the fight :
Propped on their bodkin spears, the sprites survey   55
The growing combat, or assist the fray.
  While through the press enraged Thalestris flies,
And scatters death around from both her eyes,
A beau and witling perished in the throng,
One died in metaphor, and one in song.   60
'O cruel nymph ! a living death I bear,'
Cried Dapperwit, and sunk beside his chair.
A mournful glance Sir Fopling upwards cast,
' Those eyes are made so killing '—was his last.
Thus on Maeander's flowery margin lies   65
The expiring swan, and as he sings he dies.
  When bold Sir Plume had drawn Clarissa down,
Chloe stepped in, and killed him with a frown ;
She smiled to see the doughty hero slain,
But, at her smile, the beau revived again.   70
  Now Jove suspends his golden scales in air,
Weighs the men's wits against the lady's hair ;
The doubtful beam long nods from side to side ;
At length the wits mount up, the hairs subside.

See, fierce Belinda on the Baron flies,
With more than usual lightning in her eyes :
Nor feared the chief the unequal fight to try,
Who sought no more than on his foe to die.
But this bold lord with manly strength endued,
She with one finger and a thumb subdued :   80
Just where the breath of life his nostrils drew,
A charge of snuff the wily virgin threw ;
The gnomes direct, to every atom just,
The pungent grains of titillating dust.
Sudden, with starting tears each eye o'erflows,   85
And the high dome re-echoes to his nose.

  ' Now meet thy fate,' incensed Belinda cried,
And drew a deadly bodkin from her side.
(The same, his ancient personage to deck,
Her great great grandsire wore about his neck,   90
In three seal-rings ; which after, melted down,
Formed a vast buckle for his widow's gown :
Her infant grandame's whistle next it grew,
The bells she jingled, and the whistle blew ;
Then in a bodkin graced her mother's hairs,   95
Which long she wore, and now Belinda wears.)

  ' Boast not my fall ' (he cried) ' insulting foe !
Thou by some other shalt be laid as low,
Nor think, to die dejects my lofty mind :
All that I dread is leaving you behind !   100
Rather than so, ah let me still survive,
And burn in Cupid's flames—but burn alive.'

  ' Restore the lock ! ' she cries ; and all around
' Restore the lock ! ' the vaulted roofs rebound.
Not fierce Othello in so loud a strain   105
Roared for the handkerchief that caused his pain.

But see how oft ambitious aims are crossed,
And chiefs contend till all the prize is lost!
The lock, obtained with guilt, and kept with pain,
In every place is sought, but sought in vain: 110
With such a prize no mortal must be blest,
So heaven decrees! with heaven who can contest?

Some thought it mounted to the lunar sphere,
Since all things lost on earth are treasured there.
There heroes' wits are kept in ponderous vases,   115
And beaux in snuff-boxes and tweezer-cases.
There broken vows and death-bed alms are found.
And lovers' hearts with ends of ribband bound,
The courtier's promises, and sick men's prayers,
The smiles of harlots, and the tears of heirs,   120
Cages for gnats, and chains to yoke a flea,
Dried butterflies, and tomes of casuistry.

But trust the Muse—she saw it upward rise,
Though marked by none but quick, poetic eyes:
(So Rome's great founder to the heavens withdrew,   125
To Proculus alone confessed in view)
A sudden star, it shot through liquid air,
And drew behind a radiant trail of hair.
Not Berenice's locks first rose so bright.
The heavens bespangling with dishevelled light.   130
The sylphs behold it kindling as it flies,
And pleased pursue its progress through the skies.

This the beau monde shall from the Mall survey,
And hail with music its propitious ray.
This the blest lover shall for Venus take,   135
And send up vows from Rosamonda's lake.
This Partridge soon shall view in cloudless skies,
When next he looks through Galileo's eyes;

And hence th' egregious wizard shall foredoom
The fate of Louis, and the fall of Rome.   14

  Then cease, bright nymph! to mourn thy ravished hair
Which adds new glory to the shining sphere!
Not all the tresses that fair head can boast,
Shall draw such envy as the lock you lost.
For, after all the murders of your eye,   14
When, after millions slain, yourself shall die:
When those fair suns shall set, as set they must,
And all those tresses shall be laid in dust,
This lock, the Muse shall consecrate to fame,
And 'midst the stars inscribe Belinda's name.   15

NOTES

INTRODUCTORY LETTER

Mrs. : In Pope's day grown-up ladies were all addressed as Mistress ', whether married or single.

CANTO I

1–3. The poem opens in true epic fashion. The poet addresses he Muse and tells her what is to be the subject of the inspiration or which he asks. Pope says, in effect, ' My subject, O Muse, s the consequences which sometimes result from innocent, or even ' amorous " causes, and this subject has been suggested to me by ny friend Caryll : the verses you inspire will be read by the lady Belinda, so, although the subject is a slight one, the glory of it vill not be slight if it gives satisfaction to her and to him.'

2. *contests*. The earlier version has ' quarrels '.

3. For Caryll see Introduction. In all the editions published n Pope's lifetime the name appears as ' C—— ', or ' C——l '. In iis letter to Caryll of February 25, 1714, which accompanied two copies of the enlarged edition of the poem, Pope writes : ' In this nore solemn edition I was strangely [? strongly] tempted to have et your name at length, as well as I have my own : but I remem-)ered the desire you formerly expressed to the contrary, besides hat it may better become me to appear as the offerer of an ill)resent, than you as the receiver of it.'

5. *Slight is the subject*, &c. An imitation of Virgil, *Georgic* iv. 6 :

> In tenui labor : at tenuis non gloria : si quem
> Numina laeva sinunt, auditque vocatus Apollo.

f which Dryden's translation is :

> Slight is the subject, but the praise not small
> If heaven assist, and Phoebus hear my call.

7. Dennis points out that ' compel ' is too strong a word : and Elwin thinks ' impel ' would have been better. Dennis found

every fault he possibly could with the poem especially with the management of the 'machinery'.

12. A very palpable imitation of Virgil's 'tantaene animi caelestibus irae?' (*Aen.* i. 11).

In the first edition this couplet ran:

> And dwells such rage in softest bosoms then,
> And lodge such daring souls in little men?

which was a reminiscence of a line in Addison's translation of *Georgic* iv. 83, 'their little bodies lodge a mighty soul.' Pope, says Elwin, probably altered the couplet to get rid of the stress laid by the rime on the weak word 'then'; but he retained the allusion to Lord Petre's short stature.

13–18. These six lines are a great improvement on the earlier edition, which read thus:

> Sol through white curtains did his beams display,
> And oped those eyes which brighter shine than they;
> Shock just had given himself the rousing shake,
> And nymphs prepared their chocolate to take;
> Thrice the wrought slipper knock'd against the ground,
> And striking watches the tenth hour resound.—*Pope.*

The lines were probably intended not so much to describe Belinda's waking as to be of general application. Notice that in the enlarged edition Pope gives the 'sleepless lovers' an extra two hours before they 'awake'.

17. *the bell.* A hand-bell. 'Bell-hanging was not introduced into our domestic apartments till long after the date of *The Rape of the Lock.* . . . I myself, about the year 1790, remember that it was still the practice for ladies to summon their attendants to their bedchambers by knocking with a high-heeled shoe. Servants too, were accustomed to wait in ante-rooms, whence they were summoned by hand-bells, and this explains the extraordinary number of such rooms in the houses of the last century' (Croker quoted by Elwin).

18. *the pressed watch.* There is point in this expression; for some of the early 'repeaters' were operated by pulling a string. The Rev. Edward Barlow, a Roman Catholic priest, applied for a patent for '*pulling* repeating clocks and watches' in 1686: the clockmakers opposed his claim on behalf of Daniel Quare, and the

Privy Council in March, 1687, gave judgement in Quare's favour. He had made repeaters some six years before ; and Charles II had sent one to Louis XIV. The invention was much appreciated, for it took some time and trouble to get a light from flint and tinder.

19. 'All the verses from hence to the end of this Canto were added afterwards.'—*Pope*.

20. *Her guardian sylph*. See Introduction. Belinda falls asleep again : she had opened her eyes already, line 14 ; and she definitely wakes again at line 116. It does not necessarily involve a contradiction, or the inconsistency to which Croker called attention.

23. *a birth-night beau*, i. e. a courtier at one of the balls that were given on Royal birthdays, when the dresses were of unusual magnificence.

32. *The silver token*. Silver pennies put at night by the fairies into the slippers of maids who kept the house clean (Croker).

the circled green. What are now called 'fairy-rings'. Circles of darker and longer grass, caused by a fungus. Shakespeare calls them the 'green-sour ringlets' (*Tempest*, v. 1). This was the lore taught by the nurses. The priest infused the legends of 'Virgins visited by angel-powers' (Croker).

42. *the lower sky*. See note on Canto ii. 83. 'Militia' in the sense of a military force is at least as old as 1590.

44. i. e. attend you at the theatre, and when you are driving in Hyde Park. 'The Drive in Hyde Park is still called "the Ring", though the site and shape have been changed' (Croker). 'The box at the theatre, and the ring in Hyde Park, are frequently mentioned,' says Elwin, 'as the two principal places for the public display of beauty and fashion'—and he quotes from Garth's *Dispensary*, 'Blaze in the box and sparkle in the ring.'

45. *equipage* = escort.

46. *a chair*, i. e. a Sedan chair ; in which the 'passenger' was carried by two 'chairmen', one in front and one behind, walking in step with each other.

47, 48. Pope does not follow the account of the genesis of the sylphs as given in *Le Comte de Gabalis*.

50. *earthly vehicles*. Thus Henry More, in his *Immortality of the Soul*, says : 'The Platonists do chiefly take notice of three kinds of vehicles, aetherial, aerial, and terrestrial' (Book II, chap. xiv. 1).

55. *chariots*. These were family coaches, and were still in use in the middle of the nineteenth century.

> quae gratia currum
> Armorumque fuit vivis, quae cura nitentes
> Pascere equos, eadem sequitur tellure repostos.
>   VIRG. *Aen.* vi. 653–5.—*Pope.*

56. *ombre.* See Appendix.

57–66. In making the spirits human beings who have ceased to be such, Pope is not in accord with the *Comte de Gabalis*, who assigns to them a more supernatural origin. 'The air is full of countless multitudes of nations of a human figure (Sylphs) . . . the seas and rivers are inhabited, as well as the air ; the Sages have called this kind Undines or Nymphs. . . . The earth, almost to the centre, is filled with Gnomes . . . as for the Salamanders, [they are] the inflamed guests of the Region of Fire . . . They are composed of the purest parts of the elements they inhabit.'

Elwin points out that Pope was indebted to Dryden (*The Flower and the Leaf*, line 489) for his idea of their origin :

> And all those airy shapes you now behold
> Were human bodies once, and clothed with earthly mould.

59. *termagant* = a noisy scolding woman. Originally the name of a Saracen idol in mediaeval romances, and as such introduced into the 'morality' plays, it came to be applied to any violent character. The old form of the word was Tervagant, which Skeat derives from the Latin *ter vagare*, and connects it with the *diva triformis* (Diana).

62. *elemental tea.* Elemental because made with water, the element appropriated to the nymphs, and of which, according to the *Comte de Gabalis*, they were made. *Tea* was then pronounced *tay* (cf. Canto iii. 7, 8) ; similarly *bohea* rimes with *way* in Canto iv. 153, 154. The continental pronunciation of the vowels *e* and *i* was not uncommon even down to the early nineteenth century. Lord John Russell always talked about being *obleeged* to any one.

65. *sylphs.* Here used of females : in the next couplet 'sylphs' is masculine. In the *Comte de Gabalis* the female sylphs are called 'sylphids ', and the female gnomes 'gnomids '.

70. The idea of arbitrary and temporary change of sex is again a departure from the *Comte de Gabalis* : and Elwin asserts Pope's indebtedness for both idea and phraseology to Milton, *Paradise Lost*, i. 423.

73. *spark* = lover. The word was also used as a verb in America, meaning to 'court' as a lover.

77, 78. Cf. Dryden, *The Hind and the Panther*, part iii:

> Immortal powers the term of conscience know,
> But interest is her name with men below.

Warburton says this is 'a parody of Homer'.

79. *too conscious of their face*. i.e. of their own beauty, too conceited. 'Face' should be grammatically 'faces'; this and similar licences occur several times in the poem, e.g. Canto iii. 42, 'halberts in their hand'.

81. *These*. i.e. the gnomes.

89. *a bidden blush*, i.e. rouge.

94. *impertinence* = extravagance, silliness, foolery, nonsense (Phillips's *New World of Words*, 1706), the common meaning of the word in the eighteenth century.

96. *one man's treat*. Cf. Canto iii. 169.

100. *toyshop*. The original meaning of 'toy' was 'a trifle':

> Any silk, any thread, any toys for your head.
>   (*Winter's Tale*, iv. iii. 326).

Etymologically the word is connected with *tow* and *tug*.

102. *coaches drive*. Rather an awkward expression, says Elwin, seeing that 'driving a coach' has another signification in common parlance. The turn of phrase in lines 101–2 is an echo of two lines of Statius (*Thebais*, viii. 398), a poet whose ingenious turns of expression were peculiarly attractive to Pope.

105. *who thy protection claim*. Another awkward phrase. Ariel means 'I claim the right of protecting thee', not 'to be protected by thee'.

107. *late*, i.e. lately, of late.

108. 'The language of the Platonists, the writers of the intelligible world of spirits, &c.'—*Pope*.

110. *descend* = shall descend.

115. *Shock*. Belinda's pet lap-dog. Dennis speaks of him as 'a vile Iceland cur'.

118. As Croker points out, this is rather clumsily put. He means that the first thing she saw on opening her eyes was a billet-doux, not that this was the first time she had seen one.

first opened. See note on line 20. She had not lifted her head from the pillow when she had opened her eyes before, and so had not seen the billet-doux.

119, 120. In more modern parlance *but* would be *than*. By 'wounds, charms, and ardours' he means the lover's expressions in the billet-doux.

121—end. Pope's friend, Thomas Parnell, who was staying with him at Binfield at the time, put these lines into Latin leonine hexameters, which Pope subsequently published in a foot-note. They are too long to quote here.

123 seq. As Warburton pointed out, Belinda first figures as the chief-priestess, and then as the goddess herself; the inferior priestess (line 127) being, of course, Betty. It is odd that the combing and dressing of the fateful lock is not mentioned here; but we must remember that none of these lines were in the first sketch of the poem.

130 seq. Cf. *The Spectator* for May 19, 1711: 'The single dress of a woman of quality is often the product of a hundred climates. . . . The brocade petticoat arises out of the mines of Peru, and the diamond necklace out of the bowels of Indostan.'

138. *bibles*. This is rather curious, and none of the editors seem to have noticed it. It must be remembered that all the people concerned, including Pope himself, were Roman Catholics. Possibly the word was only introduced for the sake of the alliteration, and is in the plural because all the other articles were so. It may have been suggested by its similarity to the word *baubles*.

140. *The fair*, i.e. the fair lady, Belinda.

145. 'Ancient traditions of the Rabbis relate that several of the fallen angels . . . among the rest Asrael . . . still preside over the women's toilets.'—*Pope.*

147. *plait the gown. plait* merely means to fold. The verb is derived from the substantive, which alone is found in French.

CANTO II

3. *the rival of his beams*, i.e. Belinda. Elwin contrasts this with Chaucer's 'up rose the sun and up rose Emily' (*The Knight's Tale*).

4. *Launched*, i.e. embarked, launched the boat.

'From hence the poem continues in the first edition, to verse 46, "The rest, the winds dispersed in empty air"; all after to the end of this canto being additional.'—*Pope.*

5. This line in the first edition read 'a train of well-dressed youths', &c.

18. *forget 'em all.* This was 'forgive 'em all' in the earlier version.

20. *Nourished.* Nowadays we should say 'cherished'.

25. *springes.* 'If the springe hold, the cock's mine' (*Winter's Tale*, IV. ii. 35).

'Aye! springes, to catch woodcocks' (*Hamlet*, I. iii 115).

A springe = what we call a snare nowadays, only made of horse-hair.

26. Fishermen's lines were then made of horsehair, twisted and tapering from as many as sixteen strands down to three and two, or even one. In *The Spectator* for July 13, 1711 (the year in which these lines were written), Sir Roger de Coverley is said to have 'tired many a salmon with a line consisting but of a single hair!' Similarly, we read in *Hudibras*, 'Though it be a two-foot trout, 'Tis with a single hair pull'd out.' Silkworm gut, the modern substitute, was *known,* and indeed had been used for angling purposes in the latter half of the seventeenth century (see Pepys' *Diary*, March 18, 1667); but it did not come into general use till long afterwards. The late Mr. Bowness of Bell Yard, Fleet Street, used to show an advertisement of his grandfather's dated 1760 which mentioned 'the new article, silk-worm gut'.

For line 28 Pope was probably indebted to Dryden's translation of *Persius*, Satire v, line 247; and George Buchanan has a similar line, 'et modo membra pilo vinctus miser abstrahor uno' (*Epig.* i. 44).

31. *meditates* for 'meditates over' or 'about': *meditari* is commonly so used in Latin.

34. Obviously an imitation of Virgil's 'dolus an virtus, quis in hoste requirat?' (*Aen.* ii. 390).

38. *twelve vast French romances.* Pope is not referring here to contemporary French literature, but to the romance-writers of the first half of the seventeenth century, such as La Calprenède, de Gomberville, and Mdlle. de Scudéry. In *The Spectator* for April 12, 1711, will be found a list of the books which formed the reading of a *Précieuse Ridicule*, including such works as *Le Grand Cyrus, Clélie, Cléopâtre, Cassandre,* and even the *Astrée* of D'Urfé. These heroic romances were of enormous length, extending some-times to as many as twelve volumes and several thousand pages.

39. In the original version (1712) after 'neatly gilt' there came the couplet :

> There lay the sword-knot Sylvia's hands had sewn
> With Flavia's busk that oft had rapped his own :
> A fan, a garter, half a pair of gloves, &c.

Sword-knots—see Canto i. 101—were often worked by ladies for their beaux.

46. 'Adapted from Virgil, *Aen*. xi. 795.'—*Pope*.

47. *secure*: in the sense of the Latin *securus*—free from care.

53, 54. Cf. Pope's own translation of the opening lines of *Iliad* ii and *Iliad* x.

55. *denizens*. Bishop Ken uses the word in the same figurative sense : he calls the angels 'blest denizens of light' (*Poet. Works*, 1721, I. ii). The word properly means 'a naturalized alien'.

57. *shrouds*. The word is hardly applicable to up-river light craft. The shrouds are the large ropes which support, or 'stay', the masts of a ship, and enable them to carry sail.

60. *Waft*. Notice the intransitive use of the verb.

64. *filmy dew*. Pope probably had the gossamer-spiders in his mind.

66. In this line and several others hereabouts Pope strikes up a strain of burlesque of the *Paradise Lost*.

70. *Superior by the head*. Cf. *Paradise Lost*, i. 589.

72. *begun* for 'began.' This is not infrequent in Pope: cf. *Messiah*, line 7 : 'Rapt into future times, the bard begun.'

73. *sylphs and sylphids*, i.e. male and female. This has been denied on the ground that 'sylphs had no sexes', but Canto i. 70 asserts the contrary, and undoubtedly in *Le Comte de Gabalis* *sylphid* is used to signify a female *sylph*, as *gnomid* is a female *gnome*.

75. *spheres*, i.e. spheres of action, the German 'Gebiete'.

79. What is meant by 'wandering orbs' as opposed to 'planets' it is not easy to see. Elwin suggests comets, and most editors have followed him.

81–3. These are the 'light militia of the lower sky' of Canto i. 42.

86. *glebe*, like *glaeba* in Latin, originally meant a clod of earth, and hence came to be used in the sense of any tilled land. Cf. Gray's *Elegy*, 'Their furrow oft the stubborn glebe has broke.'

90. '*And guard with arms divine the British throne*.' Wakefield

ays this was meant as a compliment to Queen Anne; but War-
urton says this was not so, and that the line was meant to be
imply a bit of ironical bombast.

91. *the fair*, i.e. the fair sex.

94. *exhale*. Here used intransitively, as was 'waft' in line 60.
o Emerson, 'When flowers reach their ripeness, incense exhales
rom them' (*Conduct of Life*; *Worship*).

97. *A brighter wash*, i.e. for the complexion, such as are men-
ioned again in line 127.

100. *furbelow*. Much the same meaning as our 'flounce', any
rnamental trimming on a petticoat. 'The pleated border of
petticoat or gown; same word as *falbala*' (N.E.D.). In *The
pectator* (No. 15) we read of 'a furbelow of precious stones, a hat
uttoned with a diamond'.

103. *slight*. Nowadays we should write *sleight*, meaning
trickery', as in the phrase 'sleight of hand'.

113. *The drops*, i.e. her ear-drops set with brilliants (Wakefield).
Note the fantastic and yet appropriate names which Pope has
nvented for the four sylphs. The Latin word *crispo* (I curl) is,
y the way, not used in that sense in Virgil. We might have
xpected that Crispissa would have been mentioned again when
he lock (her special charge) was in danger (Canto iii. 135). In
Dean Swift's *Bouts Rimés on Signora Domitilla* occur the lines:

> Dan Pope consigns Belinda's watch
> To the fair sylphid Momentilla.

116. 'This,' says Warburton in a manuscript note, 'was a fine
troke of satire to insinuate that the lap-dog is often the concern
of the fair, superior to all the charities, as Milton calls them, of
parental relation.' Compare Swift's verses on the collar of 'Tiger',
Mrs. Dingley's lap-dog:

> Pray steal me not: I'm Mrs. Dingley's,
> Whose heart in this four-footed thing lies.

119. *that seven-fold fence*. The allusion is to the seven-fold
hield of Ajax, 'Clypei dominus septemplicis Aiax' (Ovid, *Met.*
xiii. 2).

The hoop-petticoat is dealt with in *The Spectator* for July 26,
1711: 'A female who is thus invested in whalebone is sufficiently
ecured against the approaches of an ill-bred fellow.' Croker says
that the hoop-petticoats remained fashionable in Court circles till
the death of Queen Charlotte.

120. Note that *whale* = *whalebone*. Warton, by the way, in his *Essay*, quotes this line as ending with 'ribs of mail', but that is probably a printer's error.

121. *the silver bound* means the silver edging to the petticoat; probably no reference was intended to the shield of Achilles.

123 seq. Ariel, in effect, says to the sylphs, 'If any of you fails in his or her duty, or leaves Belinda unattended, he or she shall be punished by being either corked up in a bottle, or pinned on to a board, or drowned in Belinda's *Eau de toilette*, or stuck for ages in the eye of her bodkin, or clogged with ointment or pomatum, or dried up with alum like a faded flower, or broken, like Ixion, on the wheel of the chocolate mill, or be scalded in the hot frothing chocolate itself.'

126. *stopped in vials*. A vial, or phial, is a small narrow glass bottle with a glass stopper. *Vial* is historically a more correct form than *phial*, and *viol* would be better still.

128. *bodkin's*. The word *bodkin* occurs five times in *The Rape of the Lock*, and is used in three different senses.

i. Here (Canto ii. 128) it signifies a blunt-pointed needle similar to the domestic bodkin of to-day.

ii. (Canto iv. 98). Here it signifies an ornament for the head.

iii. (Canto v. 55). Used adjectivally, and signifying a sharp-pointed instrument (stiletto) similar to a tailor's bodkin of to-day.

iv. (Canto v. 88). Used as a substantive in the same sense. Readers of Scott will remember that in *The Antiquary* Lady Glenallan gives Elspeth 'a golden bodkin' to kill the child with.

v. (Canto v. 95). Signifying again a hair ornament, as No. ii.

wedged in a bodkin's eye. Pope may have had in mind the punishment of Ariel in *The Tempest*, I. ii. 271.

129. *pomatums*. *Pomatum* is a variant form of *pomade*, and means a scented ointment, said to have been made from apples originally, for application to the skin and especially to the lips. The form *pomatum* comes through the Italian forms *pomada*, *pomata*. Phillips in his *New World of Words* (1706) says, 'a sweet ointment made of the apples called Pome-waters, and Hog's lard : it is commonly used for chaps or roughness of the skin.'

131. *styptics*. A styptic is anything that is astringent, or produces contraction, and so stops bleeding, &c., from the Greek στύφειν (to contract).

132. *rivelled* = shrivelled. The word is obsolete in this sense.

The old word *rivel* meant to *wrinkle*. So Cowper in *The Task* (ii. 488) talks of 'the rivelled lips of toothless bald Decrepitude'.

133. Ixion was banished from heaven by Zeus, for base ingratitude and insolence. As he continued impenitent, Zeus struck him with his thunder, and had him tied by his hands and feet to a wheel which was continually in motion, so that Ixion's punishment was eternal.

138. *extend* = extend themselves, like troops—an intransitive use of the verb in place of the reflexive. Pope has it again in *The Temple of Fame* (265): 'And arches widen, and long iles extend.'

139. *thrid.* The word is not common. Note that it is the present tense. It is used by Beattie:

They thrid the flying maze (*Minstrel*, I. xxxv);

and by Tennyson:

He thrids the labyrinth of the mind (*In Mem.* xcvii).

CANTO III

1. 'The first edition continues from this line to verse 24 of his canto.'—*Pope.*

4. *the neighb'ring Hampton.* The manor of Hampton is mentioned in *Domesday.* At the time of the suppression of the monasteries it belonged to the Knights of St. John. Cardinal Wolsey obtained a lease from the prior in 1515, and built Hampton Court Palace, which he presented to Henry VIII in 1526. It continued to be a royal residence down to the time of George II. It was partly rebuilt for William III by Sir Christopher Wren. Mr. Hutton says (*Hampton Court*, p. 216) that in Queen Anne's reign 'it would be difficult to say whether it was better known as the home of statesmen or the resort of wits'. But Queen Anne herself was not much there. To quote Mr. Hutton again (p. 110): 'When William died, Hampton Court was the most famous of English palaces. When Anne succeeded it sank into secondary rank. Anne liked Kensington and Windsor. . . . She had no pleasant memories of her brother-in-law, nor had the place itself happy memories for her'—and he reminds us that the Duke of Gloucester (her only child who survived infancy) was born and christened there, and that she 'could never forget the anxious days when her baby hung between life and death'.

8. *tea.* See note to Canto i. 62. This line is often quoted as an instance of the grammatical figure known as *zeugma*, the use of a word in two senses at the same time. There are several other instances of it in *The Rape of the Lock*, e.g. Canto iv. 126, 'He first the snuff-box opened, then the case.'

9. In the original version this line ran:

> Hither our nymphs and heroes did resort.

11. *instructive.* The word is doubtless meant to be ironical. Originally in the first edition:

> In various talk the cheerful hours they passed,
> Of who was bit, or who capotted last.—*Pope.*

bit = hoaxed. So Thackeray (*Esmond*, III, iii): 'Miss Beatrix was quite bit (as the phrase of the day was).'

Capotted is a term from the game of picquet. If a player made all the tricks, he was entitled to count forty instead of ten, and was said to have made the capot.

17. *Snuff, or the fan.* The snuff-box of the beau and the fan of the woman of fashion are frequent subjects of ridicule in *The Spectator.* 'Women are armed with fans as men with swords, and sometimes do more execution with them' (*Spectator*, June 27, 1711).

The singular growth of the practice of taking snuff was a special feature of the reign of Queen Anne: before 1702 it was comparatively unknown. In that year vast quantities of it were brought back to England by the victorious forces of Sir George Rooke and the Duke of Ormond from Spain. It soon became very fashionable, and people used to manufacture it for themselves out of rolled tobacco with little ivory rasps which they carried in their pockets. By 1711 it had become quite customary for ladies to take it (see Steele's letter in *The Spectator* for April 4, 1712).

19, 20. The reader will remember that Belinda had not risen till noon.

Pope is here making fun of Ambrose Philips, who in his fifth *Pastoral* had the lines:

> The sun now mounted to the noon of day
> Began to shoot direct his burning ray.

Pope's *Pastorals* and Philips's *Pastorals* had both appeared in the sixth volume of Tonson's *Miscellany*, published in May, 1709.

Pope had read Philips's work with considerable attention, as is evidenced by his letter to Henry Cromwell of October 28, 1710. Some years afterwards Pope, who resented the attention which Philips's inferior work had attracted, published an ironical eulogy of it in *The Guardian* (No. 40). Philips retaliated by threatening to thrash Pope if he appeared at Button's coffee-house; and Pope went back to his old friends at Will's in consequence.

21–22. Meaning that the business of the law-courts was hurried over in order to get away in time for dinner, which in those days was at 4 o'clock in 'polite circles' (see Swift's *Journal of a Modern Lady*, written some fourteen years later).

The 'sentence' is not a document, but something that is pronounced, and so does not admit of being 'signed'. At assizes what the judge usually signs is the 'calendar', a list of all the prisoners, verdicts, and sentences; but the judge's signature has no legal effect, and nothing would happen if he did not sign it (Stone's *Justice's Manual*). Warton says line 22 is 'from Congreve', and subsequent editors have followed him. I have failed to find either the line or the sentiment in Congreve. The present poet laureate has adopted this turn of phrase in *The Season*: 'And Clara dies, that Claribel may dance.'

25. 'All that follows of the game at ombre was added since the first edition, till verse 105, which connected thus, " Sudden the board with cups and spoons is crowned." '—*Pope*.

The usual time for card-playing was after tea; about six o'clock (Swift's *Journal of a Modern Lady*). Pope here introduces the game, which was not in the original edition, before tea: for the game of ombre, see Appendix.

27. *singly :* because the ombre (Belinda) plays without a partner against the others.

30. At ombre each hand consists of nine cards. 'The sacred nine' of course means the Muses.

35. Pope adheres to his account of the origin of sylphs. See note to Canto i. 57–66.

37 seq. 'It is interesting to see from Pope's description that the coat [court] cards of his time were figured precisely as are those which are at present in use in England, or rather which were in use until the ugly but convenient fashion of double-headed kings, queens, and knaves came up' (Lord Aldenham).

38. *whiskers :* what we should now call a *moustache*, although this would not apply to the King of Hearts. In the *New World*

of Words (1706) of Edward Phillips, the word is defined as 'a tuft of hair on the upper lip of a man'. So also in Scott's *Antiquary* (chap. ix), 'He had a beard too, and whiskers turned upwards on his upper lip.'

'Whisky' in Elwin's edition is of course a misprint.

41. *garbs succinct.* Knave was the old term for a servant, and Wakefield remarks that they are represented 'in garbs succinct' because, among the ancients, domestics, when at work, had their flowing robes gathered up to the girdle about the waist (Elwin).

47 seq. 'The whole idea of this description of a game at ombre is taken from Vida's description of a game at chess in his poem entitled *Scacchia Ludus'* (Warburton); and as to this, see the Introduction.

For Spadillio, Manillio, Basto, &c., see Appendix.

her sable Matadores. All the matadors were black, because she had declared Spades as trumps.

50. In the edition (1766) which we have adopted for the text, the first word of this line is printed 'Let'—probably an error of the press.

swept the board. This expression is inaccurate here. The ombre was only said to 'sweep the board' when he won the vole. See Appendix.

54. '*plebeian card,*' i.e. what we nowadays call 'plain suits'.

57. *Puts forth one manly leg.* This is no longer true of the King of Spades, since the adoption of double-headed cards. See note to line 37.

61. *Pam.* The Knave of Clubs, the highest trump in the game of five-card loo. The word is an abbreviation of *Pamphile*, a French word for a card-game and also for the Knave of Clubs in that game. Littré derives the word from the Greek, sc. the card most acceptable to all. The name of Pam, or Lord Pam, was given to Dr. Hort, Archbishop of Tuam, by Dr. William King, Principal of St. Mary's Hall, Oxford, in his poem, *The Toast* (circa 1730), and also by Dean Swift.

loo was also spelled *Lu* and *Lue:* and the game was also known as Lanterloo, a word derived from the refrain of a popular French song of the seventeenth century. It is spelled in a variety of ways.

64. *undistinguished by,* that is, ignored as 'Pam'—nowaday we should say 'falls to' the spade.

67. *her host,* i.e. Belinda's host, objectively to 'invades'.

74. The King of Clubs is the only King that holds a globe in his hand.

76. The King of Diamonds is the only King in profile.

92. *codille*. See Appendix. If a player made more tricks than the ombre he was said to win *Codille*, and the ombre had to pay him an amount equal to what was in the pool. The word is Spanish, and may either mean ' a little corner ' or ' the arm from the shoulder to the elbow '.

93. *in some distempered state* = at some critical political juncture.

94. *nice* = critical.

95. Hearts not being trumps, the ace ranked next below the Knave. See Appendix.

100. *and long canals*. The ' long canal ' at Hampton Court is three-quarters of a mile in length and dates from Charles II.

101. For these lines see Virgil, *Aen.* x. 501 : ' Nescia mens hominum,' &c.

105. ' From hence the first edition continues to verse 134.'—*Pope*.

106. *the mill*. The ladies, says Croker, ground as well as made their own coffee, and possibly roasted it also. In a letter to Arbuthnot (July 11, 1714), Pope, describing his visit to Dean Swift at Letcombe, says : ' There was likewise a sideboard of coffee, which the Dean roasted with his own hands in an engine for the purpose, his landlady attending all the while that office was performing.'

107. *altars of Japan*. This refers to the lacquered trays.

108. *fiery spirits*, sc. spirits of wine.

110. *China's earth* = the porcelain cups. ' China,' in the sense of *ware*, was well established in Pope's day. As early as 1653, Cogan used the word in his translation of Pinto's *Voyages*, ' a present of certain very rich pieces of china.'

117. *which makes the politician wise*. A sarcastic allusion to the pretentious talk of the would-be politicians who frequented coffee-houses (Elwin).

In the above-mentioned letter (line 106) Pope says of Swift that ' he talked of politics over coffee, with the air and style of an old statesman '.

122. *Scylla's fate*. Nisus, King of Megara, had a purple lock on the top of his head, on which the safety of his kingdom depended (' magni fiducia regni '). When the Cretans besieged Megara, Scylla, the daughter of Nisus, who had beheld the Cretan leader, Minos, from a tower, and had fallen in love with him, cut off

the purple hair while her father was asleep, and took it to Minos, who was consequently victorious, but bitterly reproached Scylla with her unfilial conduct, and proceeded at once to set sail from Megara. Scylla flung herself into the sea and clung to the ship; but her father, Nisus, who had been changed into an osprey (Haliaetos), swooped down upon her, whereupon she too was changed into a bird, called *Ciris*. The story is told at length in the eighth book of Ovid's *Metamorphoses*; and in it occur the lines which Pope temporarily prefixed as a motto to the second edition of *The Rape of the Lock*.

125, 126. These two lines in the original version ran:

> But when to mischief mortals bend their mind,
> How soon fit instruments of ill they find.

Compare Dryden's *Absalom and Achitophel*, i. 79, 80:

> But when to sin our biassed nature leans,
> The careful devil's still at hand with means.

Shakespeare has the converse:

> How oft the sight of means to do ill deeds
> Makes ill deeds done (*King John*, iv. 2)

127. *Clarissa*. She has not been identified with any real person; and naturally so, unless, which would be unlikely, Lord Petre had an accomplice. Pope calls her 'a new character' in a note to Canto v. 7, &c. (q.v.). She was not 'a new character', as the present passage had existed from the beginning: Pope probably only meant that the speech (Canto v. 7 seq.) was first introduced into the poem in the edition of 1717.

132. *The little engine*. Any mechanical contrivance or tool could be called an engine. In Fuller's *Worthies* (1662), the instrument with which thieves forced open a chest is so called; and Power (1664) speaks of 'our modern engine, the microscope'. See also Pope's letter quoted in note to line 106.

134–154. 'In the first edition it was thus:—

> As o'er the fragrant steams she bends her head. Verse 134.
> First he expands the glitt'ring forfex wide
> T' inclose the lock: then joins it to divide:
> The meeting points the sacred hair dissever
> From the fair head, for ever, and for ever. Verse 154.

All that is between was added afterwards.'—*Pope*.

146. *Resigned*, i.e. resigned himself.

147. *forfex*. Latin for 'shears'.

152. 'See Milton, Lib. vi. 330, of Satan cut asunder by the ngel Michael.'—*Pope*.

154. *for ever, and for ever.* To emphasize the fact that the air could not unite again, as the bisected sylph had done.

155, 156. *flashed . . . rend*. Note the change of tense, which did not occur in the original version, where the line ran thus :

> The living fires came flashing from her eyes.

157. The original version read :

> Not louder shrieks by dames to heaven are cast.

158. *lap-dogs*. This was the word used in the original version : Pope substituted 'monkeys' in the edition of 1714, but in the 717 collected poems *lap-dogs* reappeared.

159. *China vessels.* See note to line 110

163. Pope refers, in a note, to Virgil, *Eclogue* v. 76 :

> Dum iuga montis aper, fluvios dum piscis amabit,
> Dumque thymo pascentur apes, dum rore cicadae,
> Semper honos, nomenque tuum, laudesque manebunt.

165. *Atalantis*. This was a book written by the notorious Mrs. Manley, and had for its title, *Secret Memoirs and Manners f several Persons of Quality, of both sexes. From the New Atalantis.* Two volumes of this were published in 1709, anonymously. The publishers, John Morphew and John Woodward, were arrested, nd Mrs. Manley then came forward and acknowledged the authorship. The publishers were released, and Mrs. Manley was admitted o bail in the November of the same year. Her case came before he Court of Queen's Bench, and she was discharged in the following February. At the time when *The Rape of the Lock* was written he had recently published another book, entitled *Court Intrigues, n a collection of original letters from the Island of the New Atalantis,* nd this is perhaps the book referred to by Pope. Mrs. Manley had some years before been mixed up in a forgery case, and her personality was much before the public. She apparently relied upon her friends among the Tory party, notably Dean Swift, whom she assisted as editor of *The Examiner* : though Swift in his ballad *Corinna* (1712) says :

> Her commonplace-book all gallant is,
> Of scandal now a cornucopia,
> She pours it out in Atalantis
> Or Memoirs of the New Utopia.

The *New Atalantis*, with a key to it, figures in the list of Leonora's books in *The Spectator* for April 12, 1711 (see note to Canto ii. 38). It may not be superfluous to mention that the phrase 'New Atlantis' originated with Bacon.

166. *Or the small pillow grace a lady's bed.* 'Ladies in those days received visits in their bedchambers, when the bed was covered with a richer counterpane, and "graced" by a small pillow with a worked case and lace edging' (Croker). See *The Spectator* for April 21, 1711.

171. *receives its date*, i.e. has its limit of existence fixed.

172. This line is an echo of Juvenal's 'data sunt ipsis quoque fata sepulchris' (*Sat.* x. 146).

173. *the labour of the Gods.* Troy was built by Apollo and Poseidon.

174. *the imperial towers.* The first edition had 'th' aspiring towers'.

177–8. '"Quid facient crines, cum ferro talia cedant?" Catullus 'Coma Berenices,' lxvi. 47.'—*Pope.*

CANTO IV

1. 'At Regina gravi, etc. Virg. *Aen.* iv. 1.'—*Pope.*

8. *manteau.* 'A loose upper garment, now generally worn by women instead of a straight-bodied gown' (Phillips, *op. cit.*) A Mantua gown was so called from the place. *Mantle* is an older form than *manteau*.

11. 'All the lines from hence to the 94th verse, that describe the house of Spleen, are not in the first edition; instead of them followed only these :—

> While her racked soul repose and peace requires,
> The fierce Thalestris fans the rising fires—

and continued at the 94th verse of this canto.'—*Pope.*

16, 20. **The Spleen**, an organ of the human body, was considered to be the seat of *Mirth*; and it was when this organ became disordered, usually as the result of an east wind, that the moroseness and ill-temper called 'The Spleen' were produced; and this latter sense eventually prevailed over the former. Cf.

> Cor sentit : pulmo loquitur : fel continet iras :
> Splen ridere facit, &c. (*Schola Salernitana*, Part 4).

The true function of the spleen, is, I believe, still a mystery.

17. *gnome*. See Introduction.

21, 22. Cf. Ovid, *Met.* ii. 762, of the abode of Envy :

> Sole carens, non ulli pervia vento.

24. *Megrim.* From the French *migraine* (supposed to be derived from the Greek ἡμικρανία, being a headache which only affected one half of the head).

In the original 1714 edition the word used was *Languor*, but it was altered to *Megrim* in the collected edition of 1717, and so remained.

25. *wait the throne*, i.e. wait upon, attend ; a rather strained use of the word, but Pope uses it again in *The Dunciad* (i. 265), 'She bids him wait her to her sacred dome.'

30. *lampoons.* A lampoon means any scurrilous attack on an individual. The word is French, and originally meant ' a drinking-song '.

38. *each new night-dress gives a new disease.* Nightdress, analogous to the peignoir or the tea-gown of to-day. He means that the acquisition of a new garment led to an imaginary attack of the 'vapours ', or as we should say, ' indisposition,' in order that visitors might be received *en déshabille*, and so have an opportunity of admiring the new finery.

43. *snakes on rolling spires*, i.e. erect on their coils. So Milton says of the serpent, 'erect amidst his circling spires'; *spires* of course = spirals.

46. *angels in machines.* An obsolete sense of the word 'machine', meaning a mechanical contrivance for the production of stage-effects. So Cotton in *The Wonders of the Peak* (1681) says :

> Like a machine, which, when some god appears,
> We see descend upon our theaters.

This use of the word lasted into the nineteenth century. Hood in his *Vauxhall* writes :

> Time's ripe for the ballet,
> Like bees they all rally,
> Before the machine.

The original ' machine ' was the μηχανή of the Greek theatre, a sort of crane by which the gods were introduced on to the stage as though descending from the sky, when their opportune intervention was necessary to adjust matters or solve difficulties otherwise insuperable. Hence the expression ἀπὸ μηχανῆς (Aristotle, *Poetics*). This became latinized in the phrase 'Deus ex Machina', which does not seem, however, to be found in classical Latin.

The secondary meaning of ' machine ', a supernatural person or agency introduced into a poem, and its allied word ' machinery ' meaning an assemblage of such machines (see Introduction), is not intended, I think, and should be distinguished here. Elwin's note seems to confuse the two meanings. The word ' machine ', by the way, was, in the seventeenth and eighteenth centuries, often stressed on the first syllable. Thus we have in the Epilogue to Dryden's *Oedipus* :—

> Terror and Pity this whole poem sway,
> The mightiest machines that can move a play.

Pope's two lines, 43 and 44 ('glaring fiends . . . purple fires'), were no doubt meant as an amplification of the ' dreadful ' phantoms of line 41 ; and lines 45 and 46 of the ' bright ' visions of line 42.

51. ' See Homer, *Iliad* xviii, of Vulcan's walking tripods.'—*Pope*. Pope alludes to lines 373–6 of *Iliad* xviii.

52. ' Alludes to a real fact ; a lady of distinction imagined herself in this condition.'—*Pope*.

Pope's note is all the enlightenment we have.

Geese and turkeys were made into pies. In *The Dunciad* Pope makes

> The Bishop stow (pontific luxury)
> An hundred souls of Turkeys in a pie (iv. 593, 594) ;

and *The Vicar of Wakefield* (chapter vi) says to his wife : ' I never dispute your abilities at making a goose-pie.'

53. George Steevens says that this line is an allusion to the craze of Dr. Edward Pelling, who was then chaplain in ordinary to

Queen Anne. He was a stanch opponent of Papistry, and did not die till 1718.

54. Pope seems to have taken the idea from Beaumont and Fletcher's play, *The Loyal Subject* :—

> are women now
> o' th' nature of bottles, to be stopped with corks.
>
> (Act IV, Sc. ii).

56. *healing spleenwort*. The fern referred to is probably the scaly spleenwort (*Asplenium Ceterach*), the word *Ceterach* being ' merely an adaptation of *Chetherak*, a term applied to it by ancient medical writers when discoursing of it as a cure for splenetic disorders' (F. G. Heath, *The Fern World*). 'The common name, *Spleenwort*, takes its origin in a curious story,—that in Cerito there is a river which divides two portions of land, the *Ceterach* growing abundantly on one side of the stream, and not on the other. On the side where this fern grows, the pigs are said to have no spleen, but on the other side no such deficiency is recorded, hence the name *Spleenwort* or *Asplenon*. To this day Arabian and other Eastern writers believe in the virtues of this fern in diseases of the spleen and liver' (Mrs. Lankester, *British Ferns*).

58. *rule*. This is faulty grammar for *rulest*. Similarly ' give ', ' act,' make,' &c., in the succeeding lines. This is a common slip with Pope ; cf. *The Messiah*, 5, 6 :

> oh ! thou my voice inspire
> Who touch'd Isaiah's hallowed lips with fire.

59. *vapours*. Not unlike the hysteria of to-day. The name perhaps owed its origin to the misty English climate, which was taken to be the cause of ' spleen ' and similar complaints. Cf. lines 39, 40.

69. *citron-waters*. A cordial distilled from a mixture of spirit of wine with the rinds of citrons and lemons. (Elwin).

Compare Swift's *Journal of a Modern Lady*, who wakes at noon and ' takes a large dram of citron water '.

Citron juice was also used as a toilet accessory and is included in Anstey's long list of such things in *The New Bath Guide* :—

> Bring, O bring thy essence pot,
> Amber, Musk, and Bergamot,
> Eau de Chipre, Eau de Luce,
> Sans Pareil, and Citron Juice.

71, 72. A cuckold (the husband of an unfaithful wife) was said to wear horns.

82. In the *Odyssey*, Aeolus, the king of the winds, gives Ulysses a bag in which all the adverse winds were confined. While Ulysses slept the crew opened the bag, and the ship was blown back to Aeolia.

85. *vial*. See note to Canto ii. 126.

89. *Thalestris*. This is supposed to be Mrs. Morley (the wife of John Morley, the 'land-jobber'). She was sister to 'Sir Plume' (Sir George Browne)—see Introduction. 'Thalestris was the name of the Queen of the Amazons, who went to meet Alexander the Great; a very appropriate name for a warlike woman.

91. *Full o'er their heads*, i.e. well over their heads.

98. *The bodkin*. See note to Canto ii. 128. In the original version this line read 'Combs, bodkins, leads, pomatums to prepare.'

102. 'The curl papers of ladies' hair used to be fastened with strips of pliant lead' (Croker).

The couplet 101, 102 was not in the original version, its place being there occupied by what is now the last couplet of this canto, which read, 'O! had the youth been but content to seize,' &c.

105. *Honour* is said by Elwin to mean here 'female reputation' which seems rather at variance with 'virtue' being included in the category of the next line. In the original version line 106 read 'Ease, pleasure, virtue, all, our sex resign'.

109. *a degraded toast*. Sack was often served with toast floating in it (see *Merry Wives of Windsor*, III. v. 3). It is perhaps doubtful how the word came to mean a belle whose health is drunk; but Addison tells a story in *The Tatler* (No. 24) of an occurrence at Bath in the reign of Charles II, which would seem plausible enough.

'It happened that on a public day, a celebrated beauty of those times was in the Cross-Bath, [This was the bath at the end of Bath Street, now known as 'The Twopenny Hot'.] and one of the crowd of her admirers took a glass of the water in which the fair one stood, and drank her health to the company. There was in the place a gay fellow, half-fuddled, who offered to jump in, and swore, though he liked not the liquor, he would have the toast. He was opposed in his resolution; yet this whim gave foundation to the present honour which is done to the lady we mention in our liquors, who has ever since been called a Toast.'

111. *hapless.* This word was 'helpless' in the original version of 1711, and also in the first collected edition of 1717, but 'hapless' is the word in the Warburton edition of 1766, which we have followed for the text.

114, 115. Meaning that the baron would wear the lock, or rather part of it, set in a diamond ring.

117. *Hyde-park Circus.* See note to Canto i. 44.

118. *in the sound of Bow*, i.e. 'within the sound of Bow Bells'— the bells of St. Mary le Bow in Cheapside, which figure in the story of Dick Whittington. It would have been quite out of all keeping for the *wits* of the West End to take lodgings in the City.

121. *Sir Plume.* This was Sir George Browne, the brother of Mrs. Morley (Thalestris). See the Introduction.

122. *her beau.* He was her brother.

Warburton says ' he was the only one of the party who took the thing seriously. He was angry that the poet should make him talk nothing but nonsense ; and, in truth, one could not well blame him.'

124. *nice conduct*, i.e. skilful management; the highfalutin expression is quite in keeping with the mock-heroic character of the poem.

The cane was a Malacca cane. Addison, in an amusing number of *The Tatler* (December 6, 1709), deals at length with the subject of canes and their carriage and manipulation, and introduces a gentleman carrying a cane very curiously clouded, with a transparent amber head, and a blue ribband to hang upon his wrist.

125. Spence (*Anecdotes*, 1858, p. 147) says that the lines conveyed ' the very picture of the man '.

140. *long-contended honours.* Pope took the expression from Dryden's *Epistle to Mr. Granville* (afterwards Lord Lansdowne) :

> With better grace an ancient chief may yield
> The long-contended honours of the field

141, 142. 'These two lines are additional; and assign the cause of the different operation on the passions of the two ladies. The poem went on before without that distinction, as without any machinery, to the end of the canto.'—*Pope.*

In the original version line 143 read as follows :—

> But see ! the nymph in sorrow's pomp appears,

and between lines 144 and 145 came the line ' now livid pale her cheeks, now glowing red ', forming a triplet with lines 145, 146. This trick of triplets, which Dryden employed to vary the monotony of the cadence of his heroic couplets, was seldom resorted to by Pope ; ' he admitted them, but in the opinion of Fenton, too rarely ; he uses them more liberally in his translation than his poems ' (Johnson).

'At verse 91, Umbriel empties the bag which contains the angry passions over the heads of Thalestris and Belinda.   At verse 142 he breaks the phial of sorrow over Belinda alone, whence Belinda's anger is turned to grief, and Thalestris remains indignant ' (Elwin).

156. *bohea.*   This word was derived from the Chinese Wu-i hills, whence the first black tea came to England.   In the early eighteenth century the name *bohea-tea* was given to the finest kinds of black tea ; nowadays, *bohea* means the inferior kind, the last crop of the season.   The word was occasionally stressed on the first syllable, as in Dr. Young's *Love of Fame* (vi) :—

> How too red lips affected Zephyrs blow
> To cool the bohea, and inflame the beau.

161, 168.   These lines in the original version read respectively :

> Twas this the morning omens did foretell

and

> My hands shall rend what even thine own did spare

Pope altered these, and other lines, to eliminate the expletive *did*, which was one of his aversions always.   Cf. *Essay on Criticism*, 346 :

> Where expletives their feeble aid do join
> And ten low words oft creep in one dull line.

163. *China.*   There would seem to be no reason why the word should here be spelled with a capital C.   See note to Canto iii. 110.

165, 166.   These two lines were not in the original version.

169. *sable ringlets.* ' Comparing Pope's account of Arabella's beauty with the existing portraits, it is strange that, as she is represented in all three pictures with fair auburn hair, he should have expressly described it as black ' (*The History of Ufton Court*, by A. Mary Sharp, p. 126) ; and see Introduction.

taught to break. Prior uses the word ' break' in a similar connexion :—

> thy comely tresses break
> In flowing ringlets on thy snowy neck
>
> (*Henry and Emma.*)

175, 176. These two lines in the original version occurred earlier in the poem ; see note to line 102.

CANTO V

1–6. This passage is an echo, and in places a literal translation, of the scene between Aeneas, Dido, and Dido's sister, Anna, in the 4th Aeneid.

7. *Clarissa.* 'A new character introduced in the subsequent editions, to open more clearly the moral of the poem, in a parody of the speech of Sarpedon to Glaucus in Homer.'—*Pope.*

Pope is hardly accurate in speaking of Clarissa as 'a new character', for it was she who had lent the Baron the scissors (iii. 127), a rôle she played in the original version. The present passage (lines 7–36) was not in the first enlarged version, 1714, and first appeared in the edition of 1717.

The ensuing passage—this afterthought of Pope's—embodies the moral and *raison d'être* of the whole poem, viz. the injunction to ' keep good-humour still whate'er we lose '. It is a fairly close parody, as Pope says, of the episode of Sarpedon in *Iliad* xvi, of which Pope's own translation had appeared in Dryden's *Miscellany* in 1710.

11. See note to Canto i. 130.

14. *the side-box.* The gentlemen sat in the side-boxes, the ladies in the front-box, corresponding to our ' dress-circle '. Lydia in Gay's *Toilette* exclaims :

> Nor shall side-boxes watch my restless eyes,
> And, as they catch the glance, in rows arise
> With humble bows ; nor white-gloved beaux approach
> In crowds behind to guard me to my coach.

Steele in the *Guardian* for April 14, 1713, says : 'The virgin ladies usually dispose themselves in the front of the boxes, the young married women compose the second row, while the rear is generally made up of mothers of long standing, undesigning maids, and contented widows.'

20. *the small-pox.* This much-dreaded disease in ante-vaccination days was horribly disfiguring, and left its traces on the face for life. Goethe, who had it severely, was a conspicuous exception. Lord Petre ('The Baron' of the poem) died of it before the enlarged version was published.

35. 'It is a verse frequently repeated in Homer after any speech. So spoke—and all the heroes applauded.'—*Pope.*

37. 'From hence the first edition goes on to the conclusion, except a very few short insertions added to keep the machinery in view to the end of the poem.'—*Pope.*

The other 'insertions' referred to by Pope are lines 53–56, 83, 84, 89–96, 131, 132, 135, 136.

the fierce virago. See note to Canto iv. 89. 'Virago' has not necessarily a sinister meaning: Virgil applies the word to the maiden-warrior Camilla.

42. *base.* 'bass' was so spelled, even in the nineteenth century. Sir David Brewster in *Letters on Natural Magic* (ed. 1883, ix. 288) speaks of the 'base clef'. Pope (*Dunciad*, ii. 233, 234) makes the word rime with '*ass*'.

45. 'Homer, *Iliad* xx.'—*Pope.*

47. Pope mixes up the Greek and Latin names. Pallas = Minerva; Hermes = Mercury; Latona was the mother of Apollo and Diana. The omission of the preposition before Latona is awkward.

52. From Addison's translation of *Silius Italicus,* 'and startle at the sudden flash of day.'

53. 'These four lines added, for the reason before mentioned.'— *Pope.*

'Minerva, in like manner, during the battle of Ulysses with the suitors in the *Odyssey,* perches on a beam of the roof to behold it.'—*Pope.*

A sconce is a kind of candlestick made to be hung on a wall. With a reflecting surface behind and a shield in front the light would be diffused and at the same time the glare of the flame concealed. The word is derived from *absconsus* and originally meant a concealed light; cf. the Old French *esconse*=a dark lantern.

55. *bodkin spears.* See note to Canto ii. 128.

60. Borrowed from the Duke of Buckingham's *Essay on Poetry*, where he says, of the characters of the Restoration dramatists, ' They sigh in simile, and die in rhyme ' (Elwin).

61. *a living death I bear.* It is rather difficult to see what the metaphor is.

62, 63. ' Dapperwit ' is the name of a rake in Wycherley's play *Love in a Wood* ; the name does not occur elsewhere in Pope. ' Sir Fopling' figures in the *Satires* of Donne and *The Dunciad*.

64. *Those eyes are made so killing.* ' The words of a song in the opera of *Camilla*.'—*Pope*.

The opera *Camilla, Regina de' Volsci* was composed by Marc' Antonio Bononcini, the brother of Handel's celebrated rival, the libretto being written by Silvio Stampilio. It was first produced in Vienna in 1697, and became extraordinarily popular. It was translated into English by Owen Macswinny, and produced in London in 1706, and was performed no less than sixty-four times within the next three years. In Act III, Scene iii, Tullia sings, ' Those eyes are made so killing, that all who look must die.'

65. ' Sic, ubi fata vocant, udis abiectus in herbis,
      Ad vada Maeandri concinit albus olor.
                                 Ovid, *Ep.*'—*Pope*.

The winding river Maeander (Asia Minor), now called the Menderez, has given us the modern verb.

71. ' Vide Homer, *Iliad* viii, and Virgil, *Aeneid* xii.'—*Pope*.

73. The *beam* is that part of the balance from which the scales are suspended, and hence the phrase ' to kick the beam ', meaning to be so light as to be greatly outweighed by the contents of the other scale.

83, 84. ' These two lines added for the above reason.'—*Pope*.

The *gnomes* here constitute the ' machinery ', as being the ' demons of *earth* '.

88. *bodkin.* See note to Canto ii. 128.

89. ' In imitation of the progress of Agamemnon's sceptre in Homer, *Iliad* ii.'—*Pope*.

Homer describes Agamemnon's sceptre as having been made by Hephaestus (Vulcan) for Zeus (Jupiter), and as having been owned successively by Hermes (Mercury), Pelops, Atreus, Thyestes, and Agamemnon.

95. *bodkin.* See note to Canto ii. 128. ' Pins to adorn the hair were then called bodkins, and Sir George Etherege, in Tonson's *Second Miscellany*, traces the genealogy of some jewels through the successive stages of the ornament of a cap, the handle of a fan, and

ear-rings, till they became, like the gold seal-rings in *The Rape of the Lock*,

> A diamond bodkin in each tress,
> The badges of her nobleness,
> For every stone, as well as she,
> Can boast an ancient pedigree ' (Elwin).

102. In the original version this line read ' and still burn on, in Cupid's flames, alive.'

103, 104. Imitated from Dryden's *Alexander's Feast*, lines 35, 36.

105. *Othello*, Act III, Scene iv.

113. *sphere*. See note to line 142.

114. ' Vide *Ariosto*, Canto xxxiv.'—*Pope*.

In the original version this line read, ' Since all that man e'er lost is treasured there.' Pope means by ' all things lost on earth ', things that have a fictitious value.

115. *vases*. *V*ase till the end of the eighteenth century was commonly pronounced as riming with ' base ', ' case,' &c. ; then it came to be pronounced as riming with ' phrase ', ' maze,' &c., and this pronunciation is still to be heard in London.

125, 126. Romulus was said to have disappeared during an eclipse of the sun while he was addressing the senate. To disarm suspicion, the senators caused it to be reported that he had been caught up into heaven ; the report was credited the more readily when Julius Proculus declared that Romulus had appeared to him on the road near Alba, and had confirmed this, and ordered him to tell the Romans to sacrifice to him under the name of Quirinus.

128. ' Flammiferumque trahens spatioso limite crinem
      Stella micat (Ovid).'—*Pope*.

129. *Berenice's locks*. Berenice was the sister-wife of Ptolemy III (Euergetes). She vowed the hair of her head to the goddess Venus if her husband returned victorious from Asia. He did so, and her hair was accordingly hung up in the temple of Venus. It was soon stolen, whereupon Conon, the Samian astronomer, declared that Jupiter had taken it up to heaven, and the miracle was celebrated by the elegiac poet Callimachus, of whose poems only a few fragments survive. Callimachus was the model imitated by the Roman elegiac poets, and 200 years afterwards Catullus translated the poem into Latin; and this is the well-known ' Coma Berenices ' (lxvi), with which Pope was of course familiar. See note to Canto iii. 177. The constellation known nowadays as

the *Coma Berenices* is first mentioned by Eratosthenes, who calls it 'Ariadne's hair', and afterwards, in his account of the constellation Leo, πλόκαμος Βερενίκης Εὐεργέτιδος : but its claim to a separate place among the constellations was unsettled for nearly 2,000 years, and it was first catalogued by Tycho Brahe in 1602. Only seven stars are visible to the naked eye, but Webb describes it as 'a gathering of small stars which at a sufficient distance would become a nebula to the naked eye', and Serviss says it is a 'curious twinkling, as if gossamer spangled with dewdrops was entangled there'. (See R. H. Allen, *Star Names*, pp. 168–71.)

130. *heavens.* This was 'skies' in the original version.

131, 132. 'These two lines added, for the same reason, to keep in view the machinery of the poem.'—*Pope.*

133, 134. In the original version these two lines formed part of another triplet (see note to Canto iv. 141, 142), the middle line reading :—

As through the moonlight shade they nightly stray.

The Mall, on the north side of St. James's Park, was a fashionable promenade in the evening, and continued to be so till nearly the end of the century. About two years before *The Rape of the Lock* was written, Dr. Garth, the author of *The Dispensary*, had beaten the Duke of Grafton in a flat race of 200 yards in the Mall. It was originally an enclosure, gravelled with powdered cockle-shells for playing the game of Pall-Mall (not unlike the croquet of to-day). It is now the street known as Pall Mall, 'The Mall' being confined to the gravelled walk in the park itself, which runs parallel to it.

136. *Rosamonda's Lake.* Rosamond's Pond was a sheet of water in the south-west corner of St. James's Park, 'long consecrated to disastrous love, and elegiac poetry' (Warburton to Hurd). It was the recognized place for assignations in the comedies of the Restoration dramatists. Dean Swift, in his *Journal to Stella*, speaks of it being frozen over, and 'full of the rabble sliding, and with skates, if you know what those are'. It was drained and filled up in 1770, and the name was transferred to another pond in the Green Park, which continued to be known as Rosamond's Pond down to 1840, when it too was filled up. There are several engravings in existence of the original pond ; and there was a picture of it in the exhibition of the Royal Academy in 1774.

137. 'John Partridge was a ridiculous star-gazer, who in his

almanacks every year never failed to predict the downfall of the Pope, and the King of France, then at war with the English.'—*Pope*.

Pope's mention of Partridge in 1711 gains point from the fact that Swift (writing as Isaac Bickerstaff), in his *Predictions for the year* 1708, had selected him for attack, as being one of the notorious quacks of the time. He foretold Partridge's death on March 29 in that year, and on March 30 he published a pamphlet entitled *The accomplishment of the first of Mr. Bickerstaff's Predictions, being an account of the death of Mr. Partridge the almanack-maker, on the 29th inst.*, and afterwards an *Elegy on the death of Mr. Partridge*. The Stationers' Company struck Partridge's name out of their books accordingly, and Partridge put an advertisement in the newspapers that he ' was not only now alive, but was also alive on March 29 last '.

Partridge died on June 24, 1715, a year after the publication of the enlarged version of *The Rape of the Lock*, and Pope's note, quoted above, was not added till some years afterwards.

138. *Galileo's eyes.* That is, the telescope, first used for astronomical purposes by Galileo. Milton (*Par. Lost*, v. 261) calls the telescope ' the glass of Galileo '.

142. *sphere.* This was among the words pronounced in Pope's day in continental fashion ' sphare '. It is found at the end of a line eight times in Pope, and only once (*Essay on Man*, i. 202) is it rimed otherwise.

145—end. The poem concludes, as it had opened (Canto i. 13), with a comparison of the brightness of Belinda's eyes to that of the sun.

APPENDIX

THE GAME OF OMBRE

The following remarks do not, of course, profess to be a full account either of the history or of the somewhat intricate and complicated rules of the game ; but it is hoped they will serve to enable the reader to appreciate the allusions in the text. To begin with, the word is to be pronounced as two short syllables, ombre, and not as if it were a French word. It is in fact a Spanish word, 'el hombre' (the man),[1] and means that the principal player—the ombre—the man—comes forward as a kind of challenger and undertakes to play against the other players. The game, indeed, was a development of an old Spanish game called *Primero*, and seems to have been introduced into this country by Charles the Second's queen,[2] Catharine of Braganza (to whom England also owes the city of Bombay), early in the second half of the seventeenth century. The modern name for ombre in Spain is *Tresillo*, which word has superseded the older name of *Rocamber* (much the same as our word *Rubber* in meaning) under which it is still known in Spanish South America. The game soon became fashionable, and Waller's Epigram written 'on a card that Her Majesty tore at Ombre' testifies that it was played in high circles of society. In course of time many varieties of the game developed themselves, the best known of these being perhaps *Quadrille*, which was played in at least one London club till quite the end of the nineteenth century. Lord Aldenham, whose book upon the game (privately printed, 1874) is the principal modern authority on the subject, points out that Thomas Love Peacock (or rather 'Miss Ilex'), in his story called *Gryll Grange* wrongly accuses Pope of error in his description of the game ; the mistake having arisen from her confusing Ombre with Tredille, which was a variety of Quadrille,

[1] Lord Aldenham wittily, though of course not seriously, suggested that Pope may have had the game in his mind when he penned his well-known line, 'The proper study of mankind is *man*.'

[2] A pamphlet published in London in 1660 bears the title *The Royal Game of Ombre*, but its contents are entirely political, and it does not deal with the game.

just as Quadrille was itself a development from Ombre.   Both Lord Aldenham and the writer of a most excellent paper entitled 'Pope's Game of Ombre' in *Macmillan's Magazine* for January, 1874, purport to derive their information from *The Court Gamester* of one Richard Seymour.   This was a little book which originally appeared in 1720, and was also published under the title of *The Compleat Gamester ;* it professes to have been 'written for the use of the young princesses', i. e. the daughters of the then Prince of Wales, afterwards George the Second.[1]

The game of ombre proper was played by three players and no more ;   and special tables of a triangular shape were made for it. Thus we have in Vanbrugh and Cibber's *Provoked Husband* (Act i), ' Here, get the ombre-table and the cards.'   When the household goods at Ufton Court were sold in 1770, among the contents of the ' study ' are mentioned a harpsichord, a backgammon table, and an ombre table (Miss Sharp, *op. cit.*, p. 163).

An ombre pack consisted of forty cards only, the eights, nines, and tens being eliminated.   The two black suits had no aces ; the cards which we know as the ace of Spades and the ace of Clubs being termed *Spadille* and *Basto*, and ranking respectively as the first and third trump, whatever suit might be trumps.   The second best trump was called *Manille*, and was the lowest card of whatever suit might be named as trumps by the ombre.   In the two red suits (when they were not trumps) the ace ranked next below the Knave, and was followed by the two, three, four, five, six, and seven in that order.   If, however, a red suit were trumps, the ace ranked above the King, and was called *Ponto*, being the fourth best trump.   In the two black suits the cards ranked as they do with us to-day.   Thus the order of the cards when not trumps was :

Red Suits.   King, Queen, Knave, Ace, two, three, four, five, six, seven.

Black Suits.   King, Queen, Knave, seven, six, five, four, three, two.

[1] Two editions of this book (1732 and 1734) are before me as I write, and that part of it which treats of the game of ombre is an all but verbatim translation of a little book, published in Paris, entitled *Le Jeu de l'hombre, comme on le joue présentement à la Cour et à Paris, avec les Pertintailles*.   The seventh edition of this last named (also before me) was published in 1713, so that it was more or less contemporary with the *Rape of the Lock*.

And the order when trumps was :

Red Suits. Spadille, seven (Manille), Basto, ace (Ponto), King, Queen, Knave, two, three, four, five, six.

Black Suits. Spadille, two (Manille), Basto, King, Queen, Knave, seven, six, five, four, three.

Thus, it will be seen that a red trump suit consisted of twelve cards, while a black trump suit had only eleven, because black suits had no aces.

The three first trumps (Spadille, Manille, and Basto) were called *Matadors*, from the Spanish word for 'murderer': and the peculiar privilege of the matadors was that the holder need not follow suit with them, except to a higher matador originally led. The word matador was usually extended so as to include any *sequence* of trumps headed by either Spadille, Manille, or Basto, in the hand of the ombre. This was of importance, because if all the three matadors were held by the ombre, he was paid not only for them, but also for any 'faux matadors', if he won : while, if he lost, he had to pay his opponents for each Matador (of the sequence) held by him.

Another feature of the game was that the cards were dealt and the hands played 'withershins', i. e. in the contrary direction to that usual in other games, the dealer beginning on his right. Nine cards were dealt to each of the three players, not singly but in parcels of three. This left thirteen cards to form a stock or *talon* which the dealer then placed at his right hand. The deal completed, the elder hand looked at his cards, and elected whether he would become the ombre or not ; if he declared to play, the next in order might oust him by declaring to play without taking fresh cards from the *talon*, but if he did so declare, the elder hand had a *locus paenitentiae*, and could also declare to play on his original hand—technically called playing *solo* or *sans prendre*.

If, however, the second hand 'passed', the third player had a similar option.

In this manner the ombre was determined, and the game proceeded.

If the ombre was playing 'sans prendre' (which fact *per se* entitled him to extra payments in the event of his winning), his next step was to declare what suit was to be trumps. If, however, he was not playing 'sans prendre', his next step was to 'discard' such cards as he wished and replace them by others taken from the *talon* or stock ; this done, the other two players had each a similar opportunity of amending their hands. When all had discarded, if any cards remained in the *talon*, the last discarder had the right to say whether they should be turned up or not.

The play for tricks then began. This was the same as in our modern 'whist', except that it went round from right to left, and that the three matadors were not obliged to follow suit to a smaller trump led, as already mentioned.

The dominant principle of the play lay in the fact that the other two players were quasi-partners against the ombre, and this entailed little niceties both of play and in the discard, which need not now be gone into. It is sufficient to point out that it was better for them that the strength should lie in one hand rather than be divided, for that made it more difficult for the ombre to win the majority of the tricks. The play might result in one of three ways:

1. The ombre might win more tricks than either of the other two, in which case he took the pool, and was paid for his matadors, and for playing 'sans prendre' as the case might be : or

2. One of the defenders might win a majority of the tricks, and so defeat the ombre. This was known as *Codille*,[1] and the ombre was said to be 'beasted' and had to pay the winner an amount equal to what was in the pool, the pool itself standing over for the next deal[2]: or

3. The game might be drawn, by none of the players winning a majority of tricks : in this case the ombre, having failed to make good his undertaking, forfeited to the pool the amount which it already held, so that it was doubled for the next deal.

Thus it will be seen that the pool only became emptied in the event of the ombre winning the game.

The ombre had a further privilege in the event of his making the first five tricks; he could 'venture for the vole'[3]; or, in other

---

[1] *Codille*, in Spanish, means the arm from the shoulder to the elbow.

[2] Beast, originally Beste, and pronounced as riming with 'paste', 'chaste', &c., was the word used to signify penalties incurred in certain cases by any of the players, e.g. Sir Thomas Urchard's translation of *Rabelais*, i. v, 'We will not be beasted at this bout, for I have got one trick.' The word was also the name of a separate game ; thus in *Hudibras* (iii. 1. 1007) we read of those who 'at Beste and l'ombre woo, And play for love and money too'.

[3] The word *vole* (*bola* in Spanish) is almost certainly derived from the Latin word *vola*, meaning the palm of the hand, i.e. the rest of the 'hand' after the first five tricks (the five fingers) had been won. And it is to

words, declare his intention of winning all the remaining tricks, and if he did so declare, the two defenders were allowed to see each other's hands and consult.

If the ombre won the vole he took not only the pool but all the stakes on the table ; or, as it was termed, he 'swept the Board'. This expression is inaccurately employed by Pope in Canto iii. 50. If, on the other hand, the ombre failed to win the vole, the other two players divided the whole between them.

It will be seen from what has been said that the game was played with counters. The more valuable counters were called *Fish*[1] (derived from the French word *fiche*, as 'pool' was from *poule*). The relative value of *Fish* and *Counters* varied, as might be settled by the players.

The pool was formed by each player contributing three counters whenever it became empty—and it was added to from time to time, when all three players passed, and in certain other events.

There were also ' Beasts ' or forfeits, imposed in certain cases, which also formed part of the stakes.

As already indicated, the foregoing does not profess to be a complete account of the rules or of the method of play, but it will be sufficient to enable the reader to follow the game described in Canto iii.

It is not clear whether the ombre (Belinda) was playing ' sans prendre ' or not—probably not ; that, however, would make no difference in the *play*, but only in the amount of her winnings.

The hands as played were to all intents and purposes these :—

Belinda, having declared Spades, held : Spadille, Manille (2 of Spades), Basto, King of Spades, King of Clubs, King of Hearts, Queen of Hearts, and two small Diamonds.

The Baron held : Queen of Spades, Knave of Spades, three small Spades, King of Diamonds, Queen of Diamonds, Knave of Diamonds, and the ace of Hearts.

The *third player* (the dealer) held : two small Spades, Knave of Clubs (Pam), a small Club, Knave of Hearts, and four small Hearts.

Belinda's hand, it will be seen, is very strong, and her declaration of Spades is quite right. The Baron's, such as might fairly justify

be noted that Rabelais, who used *vole* for the palm, uses the word *voler* in the sense of losing (not winning) the vole.

[1] Christopher Anstey, in his *New Bath Guide*, speaking of the lady gamesters at Bath, calls them

 ' Industrious creatures ! that make it a rule
  To secure half the Fish, while they manage the Pool.'

him in hoping to win *Codille*. The Dealer's, very weak, which was all in the Baron's favour, for, as already explained, it was better for the defenders to have the strength in one hand, rather than distributed between the two.

We will now follow the play of the hands as detailed in the poem (lines 49-98), calling the third player the Dealer, for so he was. The lead is with Belinda, who plays *Spadille*, and the Baron and the Dealer each follow with a small trump (Spades). She then leads *Manille*, and the same thing happens. Her third lead is *Basto*, to which the Baron plays another small trump, and the Dealer (not holding any more) plays any small card—say his small Club. Belinda now holds the leading trump, the King of Spades, and can place the remaining two (the Queen and the Knave) in the Baron's hand. She leads the King, the Baron plays his Knave, and the Dealer (who is left with the Knave of Clubs, and the Knave and four small Hearts) discards—according to the poem—the Knave of Clubs (Pam). This was obviously right play.

Belinda has now made four tricks, and only requires one more to win the game. She knows that the remaining trump (the Queen) is with the Baron, but she does not know what his other four cards may be. She herself holds the King of Clubs, the King and Queen of Hearts, and two small Diamonds: she is justified in supposing that the Dealer has probably no more Clubs, since he has discarded the Knave, therefore it is the more likely that the Baron has at least one. If she can make her King of Clubs, the game is hers; she accordingly leads it. Alas! The Baron trumps it with his Queen of Spades; the Dealer discarding. The Baron now has the lead, and can bring in his long suit (Diamonds). He leads the King, the Dealer discards again, and Belinda follows suit with a small one. The Baron then plays the Queen of Diamonds, and the same thing happens. Then the Baron leads the Knave of Diamonds, the Dealer again discards, and Belinda, left with the King and Queen of Hearts, plays the latter. Everything now depends upon whether the Baron holds another Diamond, as well he may, seeing that the Dealer has discarded so many Hearts: if it be so, Belinda must lose *Codille*, and will have to pay an amount equal to what is already in the pool, as well as be beasted for all her four matadors. Fortune, however, favours her: the Baron leads the Ace of Hearts which ranks next below the Knave (Hearts not being trumps): the Dealer follows suit with his remaining Heart, and Belinda's King

Falls like thunder on the prostrate Ace.

INDEX

THE END

PRINTED IN
GREAT BRITAIN
AT THE
UNIVERSITY PRESS
OXFORD
BY
JOHN JOHNSON
PRINTER
TO THE
UNIVERSITY